FIRST PRINCIPLES OF VERSE

First Principles of Verse

By
ROBERT HILLYER

Boston
THE WRITER, INC.
Publishers

FOREWORD

As I said in the Note to the first edition of this work, it does not plumb the depths that underlie the infinite variety of English rhythms. A book much longer than this could be devoted to paeonic verse alone, or to the interplay between accent and time, or to any one of a score of prosodic matters, and still leave the subject further from exhaustion than the reader. Versification is a field loud with controversy and hazy with conflicting theories. This present volume aims merely to give the reader and the would-be poet a series of clear, indisputable guides to short cuts both in appreciation and practice.

Reading over my chapters with a view to the new edition, I considered the possibility of recasting them in more formal style, but decided against it. On the contrary, I wrote the new parts in harmony with the informal ease of the old. I have always believed that sombreness is more usually a sign of mud than depth, and that the ocean is no less impressive for a play of light on its surface.

Some of my old friends and pupils may wish to know just what changes I have made. In the first place, although I have not reprinted Miss Mildred Boie's grace-

ful Foreword, which was clearly intended for a debût,
I am always grateful to her for persuading me to the
project. The first two chapters ("Diction" and "The
Music of Words") have been slightly revised. Chapter
3 ("Metre") has been added to and changed in one
fundamental principle respecting the use of blank verse
by beginners. Chapter 4 ("Basic Metrical Forms") has
been completely rewritten. Succeeding chapters have
all been revised to a greater or lesser degree except for
the section on poems for analysis ("The Workshop")
which stands much as it was. These examples did not
need much revision, for they remain illustrative, and
the comments are based on principles that do not
change. The essay, "Some Roots of English Poetry," has
been omitted, and in its place I have included, with
the gracious permission of the editor of *The Atlantic
Monthly,* where it first appeared, an essay, "On Reading
Verse Aloud," which seems to me of primary im-
portance.

Lastly, I have added a double Reading List, general
for the subject and specific for the separate chapters.
For this list I have made reference to those indispensable
anthologies, the revised *Oxford Book of English Verse,*
edited by Sir Arthur Quiller-Couch, and *Modern
American Poetry* and *Modern British Poetry,* edited
by Louis Untermeyer. I recommend to all readers, even
if their point of view be from criticism only, the com-
position of brief exercises in the various forms of verse
which are discussed. With this advice in mind, I have

felt at liberty to address all my readers as fellow-poets, at least in aspiration.

For some reason, many people who know nothing concerning the principles of the art of verse yet feel confident to pronounce upon it. The same people would hesitate to push ignorance to dogmatic lengths in regard to the sister arts of painting or music. Verse is a technique as delicate as orchestration. It requires some knowledge of detail and structure for its full enjoyment. I have tried to provide that knowledge with as little fuss as possible.

As a textbook, these pages provide ample material for a half-year course. Every week an exercise in verse would be desirable as well as a careful technical analysis of the selections suggested for each chapter. The more general list may be used as collateral reading and should be completed by the end of the half-course. It will then prove sufficiently extensive to serve as a background for a survey course in poetry in the second half-year.

Specialists are prone to delight in the mumbo-jumbo of their subject. In avoiding this temptation, I have used as few technical terms as possible. There is no sense in wasting pages on a glossary to turn back into simple English what could originally have been expressed that way. Such practices are like the waste of time, machinery, and paper which goes into making sugar lumps and wrapping them up individually, merely that the consumer may rasp his fingernails tearing the paper off again and crack his knuckles breaking those appalling little slabs of marble in two, one half to be used, the other half, along with all the time, patience, and paper, to be wasted. Pedants and their jargon are like that, except for the sweetness.

Nor have I encumbered my pages with many charts. Any rhyme-scheme which I have omitted as not essential may be found in the dictionary, a volume I have no intention of duplicating. Metrical diagrams, except for elementary illustration, are almost useless. There is no system of notation in existence which would not be confusing beyond reason. Music, the Classical foot, the Anglo-Saxon accent and two-fold line, French forms, are all in our verse, together with differing lengths of vowel sounds and pauses, intensity of consonant sounds, degrees of accent, extra syllables, pitch, hiatus,—but we must stop somewhere. All these would have to be indicated. They may all be recognized in analysis, but the only way to hear them and compose them harmoniously is by long familiarity with the way they sound in the works of the masters. No one can write verse who has not already a large measure of familiarity with the work of his predecessors. It is important to analyze lines and passages for oneself, but to pore over analyses formulated by others is like looking at a sheet of music without hearing anything. No handbook can be a substitute for experience. I hope all my readers have, or will soon acquire, a stock of good poetry to which they can refer the comments in this book.

The volume, then, is a guide to accepted English and

American poetic technique. Much, however, that is being published today in the guise of poetry is widely experimental, narrowly obscure, and highly dubious. To that door I have no key, so can offer the reader none. It is not probable that much remains lost behind doors opening on vacuity.

It is customary at the end of a foreword to express thanks individually to those who have helped the author. I am unable to perform this amiable duty only because the number of my collaborators and hearteners is so great. The roster of my pupils, past and present, is as ample as their encouragement. Furthermore, this book in its original form was distributed throughout the camp libraries during the war, and among many correspondents from the field and the ships, some have remained as friends and fellow-poets. To those and my former students at Harvard, Radcliffe, Trinity, Kenyon and my non-collegiate pupils as well, scattered throughout the country and the pleasant decades, I send my thanks and greetings.

ROBERT HILLYER

CONTENTS

FIRST PRINCIPLES OF VERSE

DICTION

OUR concern in this present study is not Poetry—which is undefinable—but versification, which must be studied by anyone who would compose poetry or appreciate it fully. Poetry is the spirit; technique is the substance.

From the technical standpoint no poem is stronger than its weakest word. A large proportion of the words in any language imply a significance quite apart from their literal meaning as recorded in the dictionary. These secondary meanings we call overtones or suggestions, and it is in the deft manipulation of overtone that the poet finds the largest possibilities for exerting his skill with words. "Wisdom lies in masterful administration of the unforeseen," said Robert Bridges, and nothing could be more unforeseen than the tricks which words can play on us.

Let us take a compound without any overtones whatever: *lamp-shade*. This is a "flat" word, yet it is formed from two words which have strong overtones. Consider the secondary meanings implied by the word *lamp*, by the word *shade*. To go further, take the word *rose*. I would venture a guess that nine times out of ten when a poet uses this word he means not the common or garden variety of rose, but that unimaginable flower which suggests passion, love, the ephemeral quality of earthly desire, or, as the *rosa sine spina,* the Queen of Heaven herself. And finally, consider the word *cross.* To the Roman subject of two thousand years ago, cross merely brought to mind an instrument of death. It was the guillotine, the electric chair, of the period. Yet so closely has this word become associated with the greatest of the crucified, that it has lost its basic meaning completely, and has become a *symbol.* Between *flat words* and *symbols,* there lies an infinite variety of significance which the poet must learn to harmonize as skillfully as the composer harmonizes his instruments.

Bad verse has depended too much on rich words, or words with overtones, and on abstract words which seem to mean much more than they actually do. A familiar example of this weakness is often found in invocations to abstract *Beauty.* The poet professes to swoon before the lady, yet is either too lazy or too unobservant to tell what she looks like. He hopes that the one word, *Beauty,* with its obvious overtones, will do the trick that he is not skillful enough to perform. Here is an example of this sort of writing from a recent magazine:

> . . . Life's Mystery,
> Who in some wonder-star
> Singest thy spirit song,
> O Beauty, be not far!

From my own experience, I should judge that anything as vague as a "wonder-star" would be very far indeed. This reliance upon words which are blurred rather than heightened by their secondary meaning has produced a hackneyed, indefinite, and highly artificial language which is called "poetic diction." The following words too frequently fall into this class, though I should be the last to say that they belong to it of necessity: *flames, desire, lily, star, heavens* (for sky), *ethereal, eternity, spirit, ecstasy, infinity, weird, soul, heart.*

I have said that these words, and hundreds of others like them, are not necessarily "poetic diction." They may be redeemed if they are employed again in their literal sense. One of the many tasks which poetry has to perform is the continual promotion from the ranks of words which have hitherto been flat. If it fails to perform this task, and depends on the grizzled veterans who have served it too long already, its campaign is weakened. Retire the words which have worked too long and have gone stale, or else *assign them new duties.* There is no verbal effect stronger than the old word in a new place, as long as eccentricity is avoided. Emily Dickinson's choice of words is admittedly one of the greatest charms of her poetry, and her choice more often than not falls on words which have become "poetic" in the bad sense. But she has assigned them new duties:

> There is a solitude of space,
> A solitude of sea,

A solitude of death, but these
Society shall be
Compared with that profounder site,
That polar privacy
A Soul admitted to itself:
Finite Infinity.

Note the words which have become worn to a shadow
of themselves in the service of minor verses: *solitude,
space, death, polar, soul, infinity.* Yet in this poem they
are revealed in a new strength, a new freshness, because
they are performing a duty which the poets have not
permitted them to perform for years; they are back to
their basic meaning. Note, too, how the rather flat
words, *society, site, admitted,* and *finite,* shoulder their
new responsibility in the presence of their elders and
give forth the suggestions demanded of them. So far,
then, we have seen that the diction of poetry should be
simple, definite, and fresh.

It is well, also, to show restraint, to keep our diction
at a low intensity. Then when we wish a sudden flight,
the contrast will fulfill our purpose. Rhapsodic effects,
and particularly invocations and apostrophes, should be
reserved for their inevitable place in passages heightened
by the greatest intensity of awe. Consider how much
restraint in diction contributes to the fine tragedy of
Rossetti's "Woodspurge"—a tragedy finer for being
irrevocable:

The wind flapp'd loose, the wind was still,
Shaken out dead from tree and hill:

I had walk'd on at the wind's will,—
I sat now, for the wind was still.

Between my knees my forehead was,—
My lips, drawn in, said not Alas!
My hair was over in the grass,
My naked ears heard the day pass.

My eyes, wide open, had the run
Of some ten weeds to fix upon;
Among those few, out of the sun,
The woodspurge flower'd, three cups in one.

From perfect grief there need not be
Wisdom or even memory:
One thing then learnt remains to me,—
The woodspurge has a cup of three.

Exactitude of diction, however, may have to be sacrificed to a higher aim: exactitude of thought. It may be that we wish to express an idea which demands for its expression the blurring of an image. Take the familiar simile from "Adonais":

Life, like a dome of many-coloured glass,
Stains the white radiance of Eternity.

A literal minded reader, too insistent on concrete image, might insist that Shelley enumerate the colors, whether they were red, green, and violet, or purple, blue, and gold. He might contend that the dome does not become visible. But the poet's aim was not the portraying of the dome, it was the swift embodiment of an abstract idea. Had he continued in his description, the emphasis would have shifted from the thought to the image, and all the values of the poem would have been falsified. Hence, he telescoped his meaning in the words *many-coloured* and *stains*. Some years ago, a school self-styled the Imagists set forth several rules for the guidance of poets, among which they declared that poets should always employ the "exact" word. Yet they noted the limitations of such a rule, and added that they meant not the exact word in relation to an individual figure in a poem, but in relation to the mood of the poem as a whole. For they found, as all poets must, that the main intention of a work bends every phrase to its use.

Note well, however, that the diction of poetry must never be generally ignoble, because the intention can not be. Although every subject in the world is open to poetic treatment, poetry by its very nature exalts everything it touches. It exalts, it intensifies, it condenses. If a sordid effect be conveyed by a poem, there has been a grave mistake somewhere; or if, as in the case of most newspaper verse, a platitude remain a platitude, nothing has been gained by putting it into verse form. In this process of heightening, diction plays a major role. That is why there can never be properly, a "poem in slang." For if a constant use of "poeticisms" spoils the effect of a poem, no less certainly does flat or vulgar diction spoil it at the other extreme. The use of slang in verse defeats two important aims: it prevents elevation of the theme, and it limits the possibilities of survival. Slang shifts constantly, and the slang verses of today will be incomprehensible twenty-five years from now.

The intention of the poem as a whole will be further thwarted if our diction is uneven. Thus padding should be strictly avoided; adjectives should be chosen with scrupulous care and reduced in number; verbs should move actively, as is their function. On the other hand, we should not by a too-clever word or phrase mar the unity of the poem as a whole. When Byron writes:

> But—Oh! ye lords of ladies intellectual,
> Inform us truly, have they not henpeck'd you all?

we pause over the conspicuously clever rhyme words,— as he intended us to. But when Hood, in the last stanza of "The Bridge of Sighs," writes:

> Owning her weakness,
> Her evil behaviour,
> And leaving, with meekness,
> Her sins to her Saviour!

we pause over the *behaviour-Saviour* rhyme,—perhaps even with admiration of its cleverness,—and the whole effect of the poem is destroyed in the crucial stanza. For the poet's intention was not to reveal the resources of his vocabulary but to move us with pity for the "one more unfortunate." I have chosen an example where the fatal slip occurred on the rhyme word, because it is the most conspicuous, but in the body of the line we must be no less careful.

Another foe to smooth diction is a sudden change of tone, unless that is exactly the effect desired. Wordsworth certainly had no idea of being funny when he wrote:

> What fond and wayward thoughts will slide
> Into a lover's head!
> "O mercy!" to myself I cried,
> "If Lucy should be dead!"

Yet we laugh just where we are supposed to have at least an inclination toward tears. The verb *slide,* with all its inappropriate overtones, is unfortunate, and with the *"O mercy!"* the poem collapses into bathos. Yet in E. A. Robinson's "Richard Cory," where a grim and ironic effect is intended, the device works perfectly:

> Whenever Richard Cory went down town,
> We people on the pavement looked at him:
> He was a gentleman from sole to crown,
> Clean favored and imperially slim . . .
>
> And he was rich—yes, richer than a king—
> And admirably schooled in every grace:
> In fine, we thought that he was everything
> To make us wish that we were in his place.
>
> So on we worked, and waited for the light,
> And went without the meat, and cursed the bread;
> And Richard Cory, one calm summer night,
> Went home and put a bullet through his head.

The effectiveness of that prosaic last line is wholly attributable to the restraint in diction of the lines preceding it. Suppose the last stanza had been written thus:

We toiled and yearned toward Heaven's starry light,
And viands lacking, broke our wheaten bread;
When lo! great Richard 'neath the vernal night
Went home and put a bullet through his head.

May the author of "Richard Cory" forgive the admirer
who has dealt with him in this manner!

The diction of poetry should be simple, restrained,
definite, appropriate, and—natural. In the first place,
keep your words in their natural prose order unless you
have in mind a definite effect, such as emphasis, which
can be gained by inversion. Do not allow the exigencies
of either rhyme or metre to force your sentences into an
unnatural form. Rhyme, metre, and natural order can
all be combined—if you are willing to work long
enough. Do not employ archaic or obsolete expressions
unless (and this exception applies to all suggestions)
there is something to be gained by them which will
contribute to your general purpose. And do not employ
artificial abbreviations such as *o'er, 'neath, 'mid, e'er,
e'en, th',* and the myriad other similar follies which we
have inherited from the syllable-counting seventeenth
century. Generally your metre will welcome the extra
syllable. In the rare cases where it does not, look for a
synonym.

There is no better way of summing up than to give a
practical example. Masefield's sonnet "The Lemmings"
is good enough to sustain analysis without injury:

1   Once in a hundred years the Lemmings come
2   Westward, in search of food, over the snow,

3   Westward, until the salt sea drowns them dumb,
4   Westward, till all are drowned, those Lemmings go.
5   Once, it is thought, there was a westward land,
6   (Now drowned) where there was food for those starved
       things,
7   And memory of the place has burnt its brand
8   In the little brains of all the Lemming Kings.
9   Perhaps, long since, there was a land beyond
10 Westward from death, some city, some calm place,
11 Where one could taste God's quiet and be fond
12 With the little beauty of a human face;
13 But now the land is drowned, yet still we press
14 Westward, in search, to death, to nothingness.

The idea of this sonnet rides firmly. We begin with the lemmings, mysterious though actual rodents which from time to time are seized with a communal mania and rush westward in thousands, to fling themselves into the sea.

The poet lifts his idea slowly to a symbolic meaning: it is the soul of Man always searching for his Eden, his Avalon, his Isles of the Blest, his Atlantis—the lost land lying to westward. One small shift in the person of the pronoun gives the cue to the idea: the shift from the third person of line 1 to the first person of line 13, through the indefinite *one* of line 11. Two words, we note, recur several times, *drown* and *westward*. We note that in lines 2 and 3 these words are used as "flat" words—literally. But with each repetition they take on overtones from the context, until in line 13, *drown,* having practically lost its literal meaning, stands for all the frustration of our human life, and in line 14, *westward* has become a symbol for that Paradise toward which Man pushes in enduring hope in spite of failure.

One of the commonest forms of poetical expression consists of an image, or a picture, related to personal emotion. Shelley's "Ode to the West Wind," Keats's "Ode to a Nightingale," and scores of other great poems, particularly since the Romantic Movement, fall into this pattern. The first four stanzas of Keats's ode are largely devoted to the poet's mood; the next three, in general, to the images of the night and those called forth by the bird's song; and the last, again, is largely subjective. In Shelley's "Ode to the West Wind," the division is sharper. Although the refrain "O hear!" prepares us for the emotional climax to come, that climax is deferred through three of the quatorzains, begins to rise in the fourth, and bursts in full power at the end of the fifth and terminal stanza.

Studying these two poems, we deduce two principles for the composition of verse wherein description and feeling are combined. If the two elements are somewhat interwoven, they must be maintained at exactly the same intensity—in the same key, as it were— throughout the poem. Furthermore, their expression must be so attuned that we shall not feel any jolt as the poet passes from objective description to subjective emotion. But if, as in Shelley's ode, the two elements are distinctly separated, the emotion following and crowning the description, then there must be a perceptible rise toward a climax through the whole work.

We could take Rossetti's "Woodspurge" (on pages 6 and 7) to illustrate the first type wherein emotion and description are blent, and Robert Bridges' "The Evening Darkens Over" to illustrate the rise to a dramatic climax:

> The evening darkens over
> After a day so bright
> The windcapt waves discover
> That wild will be the night.
> There's sound of distant thunder.
>
> The latest sea-birds hover
> Along the cliff's sheer height;
> As in the memory wander
> Last flutterings of delight,
> White wings lost on the white.
>
> There's not a ship in sight;
> And as the sun goes under
> Thick clouds conspire to cover
> The moon that should rise yonder.
> Thou art alone, fond lover.

Contrast with the meditative quality of Rossetti's poem the dramatic surprise at the end of Bridges'. Here the gradual darkening of the tone, the introduction of a slightly sinister quality, and the increasing simplicity of the diction, prepare the way for the climax in the last line.

Many poems which attempt this subtle relation of humanity and nature are marred, when they interweave description and mood, by pathetic fallacies and, frequently, a sentimentalization of the material. When a climax of mood is attempted, too often the authors fail to intensify the emotion toward the end. They must still learn that increased simplicity is nearly always the most effective preparation; that fervid phrases and too personal revelations must always destroy the power of their work. In the following verses, these faults are particularly disappointing because the first stanza, embellished with more than one memorable line, is excellent:

THE SLEEPING PRINCESS

(from Hans Christian Andersen)

Here is the garden where she lies asleep,—
Even the lilies are afraid to weep,
And the wild roses would not dare to creep
And touch her hand!
The nightingale dreams on his last high note;
Hushed is the skylark's silver-fluted throat;—
The sunlight drowses heavy on the moat,
Silent the land!

The last four lines of this stanza beautifully convey the idea of the sleeping country. The image is well expressed. The second stanza begins well enough, but then, instead of simplifying, the author complicates the emotion with all sorts of meaningless abstractions, "fillers" dictated by rhyme: *ecstasy, eternity*. Will our writers not omit these words for a while? They have been sorely overworked, and if they are ever to be of any use again, they must have time to catch their breath!

Only my heart is beating wildly fast,—
Love, can it be a hundred years have passed,
Or did your lips in touching mine, at last
Kiss Time to rest?
Death was the hour that you went from me;
Life is to hold you close in ecstasy,—
And this one moment brings eternity,
Here on your breast!

A far cry from the simplicity of "Thou art alone, fond lover."

CHAPTER 2

THE MUSIC OF WORDS

Pɪᴛʏ the poor versifier who, having chosen the exact word for his thought, believes that his technical equipment is complete. His verbal task is less than half accomplished. For in poetry we must consider not only the overtones of meaning conveyed by a word, but also the overtones of sound.

Let us admit at once that the true music of words can not be analyzed, taught, or learned. The feeling for it abides in the natural ear of the writer, and if that sensitiveness to appropriate sound be lacking or false, then the ear is not the ear of a poet. A mere delight in sonorous sound may not indicate the working of a poetic ear; the true artist is sensitive to every kind of sound and will employ those that are abrupt and jagged as well as those that are melodious—each in its proper place. Our orchestra must have not only violins, harps, and 'cellos, but drums, cymbals, and trumpets as well.

Walter Pater's remark to the effect that all the arts tend toward music applies particularly to poetry—the poetry of emotion and mood. All of us have at some time experienced an emotion too vague to be expressed in a definite verbal formula, which has, nevertheless, suggested a phrase or a sentence harmonious with it. Even people not poets share this experience; in moments of extreme joy or sorrow they babble over and over again words which at the time seem of significance, but recalled later, in a different mood, are patently nonsense. Or sometimes in a dream, verses occur to us which seem heavenly utterance, so vast, so exquisite is their meaning. Robert Bridges gives a dignified expression to this experience:

> I too will something make
> And joy in the making;
> Although tomorrow it seem
> Like the empty words of a dream
> Remembered on waking.

Then there is Shakspere's couplet:

> Thus have I had thee, as a dream doth flatter,
> In sleep a king; but waking, no such matter.

Now, most of the moods and emotions which find expression in poetry are of the nature of dreams. They take possession of all our faculties, suspending those which are not in sympathy with them. We note in passing that the Puritans, who never allowed themselves to be possessed by any mood, who fought off any emotion, good or evil, produced very little poetry. It is essential that the poet run the spiritual risk of yielding completely to the impulse which is trying to make him its instrument, for if he hold back, if he stint his inspiration, either through caution or through the knowledge that it is lunch time and he is hungry, then he is not the single-toned lyre that he must be. The many conspicuous moral failures among artists of all sorts do not indicate that the makers are less responsible than other men, but merely that they have taken more than the usual risk and have not always come through unscathed. Shelley's invocation "Make me thy lyre even as the forest is," was not empty rhetoric; it was the yea-saying of a spirit desperately in earnest.

Where the mood leaves off, artistry must begin. We can not, like the man in the dream, leave the mood to dictate the form as well as the content of our poem. Once in a great many years a poem is produced in this manner by a genius with whom technical excellence is instinctive. The supreme poem of unedited mood is, of course, Coleridge's "Kubla Khan." Here the music is perfect, the images inevitable, and we ask no more of the poem than that it possess us with its literally meaningless incantation even as the original mood possessed Coleridge. There are other fragments of the same sort, such as Hamlet's quatrain:

> Why, let the stricken deer go weep,
>   The hart ungallèd play;
> For some must watch, while some must sleep:
>   So runs the world away.

Here there is no "message" for the literal-minded, but anyone with an ear for the music of words will not fail to catch the weary melancholy, the wistfulness, which cry out from these lines as they might cry out from the *adagio* of some fine symphony. Furthermore, the lack of exact meaning is a shrewd index to the excitement and inarticulateness of Hamlet's distracted mind. Another example, which combines incantation with an ordered symbolic meaning, is Blake's "Sunflower":

> Ah, Sunflower, weary of time,
>   Who countest the steps of the sun;
> Seeking after that sweet golden clime,
>   Where the traveller's journey is done;
>
> Where the youth pined away with desire,
>   And the pale virgin shrouded in snow,
> Arise from their graves, and aspire
>   Where my Sunflower wishes to go!

The symbolic meaning of the poem is obviously the yearning of earth-rooted flesh for the moving sun of Eternity, but we need no verbal key to that meaning, for the music conveys it.

I quote these passages not to incite the reader toward what we might call the subconscious method of composition. We are not Coleridges, Shaksperes, or Blakes. Poems like those are exceptions to the general rule that *in expressing a vague mood our diction must be as definite as possible.* Poe failed miserably when he tried to employ abstract music for the expression of an abstract mood. In "Ulalume," the deliberate attempt to employ words as mere music bores the reader. "The Raven" is better, but even this poem would gain immeasurably by a slight shift to more familiar mental territory. Fol-

lowing Poe, the French "Symbolists" and their follow-
ers go to the extreme of doing away completely with all
semblance of literal meaning; they give us no con-
nected images, no ideas, merely a flow of sound which,
in their estimation, will reawaken in us the sensations
incident to the composition.

At the present time, the magazines are full of verses
which are justified neither by their music nor by their
idea. The notion is prevalent, apparently, that a com-
plete lack of thought can be compensated for by a
pretty lilt or a sonorous word. I have already spoken
against the use of abstract words, and that is a warning
which can not be too often repeated. *Eternity,* for in-
stance, is a very harmonious word indeed, but no poet
has the right to use it unless he means it in its full sig-
nificance—and, in this temporal existence, such occa-
sions are rare. No music but *perfect* music can make
up for a meagreness of intellectual content. Hence, the
good lyric should not only sing well, it should also
have something to say, and in most cases we soon dis-
cover that the simplest method of saying is also the
most melodious way of singing. There is an Eliza-
bethan lyric which has always seemed to me without a
flaw. The emotional content is not large, to be sure,
but it is set forth so simply, so naturally, that we al-
most hear the melody to which it was sung:

> Weep you no more, sad fountains;
> What need you flow so fast?
> Look how the snowy mountains

Heaven's sun doth gently waste.
But my Sun's heavenly eyes
View not your weeping,
That now lies sleeping
Softly, now softly lies
Sleeping.

As I said in beginning our discussion, there is no law by which such melody can be achieved. It is the product of a naturally musical ear developed by the continual consciousness that lyric poetry must be song. It is the golden mean between poetry too starched with idea and poetry too flimsy from the lack of it. We read Tennyson more for his music than his thought, Browning for his thought more than his music, Shakspere for music and thought of equal nobility, equal grandeur. And to those who have not the experience of these poets, we would recommend an aspiration toward clear thought as well as clear sound, so that if our melody fail of perfection, at least something will be left to make the poem worth reading.

Some elements of the music of words can be taught: alliteration, assonance, and rhyme.

There are adornments which, though not essential, have so grown into the technique of verse as to be almost indispensable.

Alliteration

Alliteration is the most ancient of our devices for enriching verse and is the characteristic of Anglo-Saxon poetry. In that poetry, alliteration followed a set pattern. The line in Anglo-Saxon verse consisted of four beats divided into two cadences of two beats each, separated by a pause. The initial consonant of the third beat set the alliterative pattern of the line. The fourth beat was, as a rule, not alliterated. The first beat or the second beat or both of them matched consonant sounds with the third. Thus, in Meredith's "Love in the Valley" we have an almost perfect modern example of Anglo-Saxon pattern with the alliteration on the second and third beats:

Shall the birds in *v*ain then X *v*alentine their sweethearts.

The set system of alliteration gradually vanished from our technique as rhyme was introduced from France. We have abandoned the pattern and employ the device irregularly to enhance the quality of our music. There is only one law which can be laid down in this connection: Do not overwork alliteration. A very little, subtly introduced, is all our rhymed and metred verse will endure without protest. Milton, who was a master of alliterative effects, sometimes employs them much more emphatically than we should dare to do. For example:

> . . . most musical
> Most melancholy nightingale.

Swinburne, who in so many ways was a master of harmonious language, marred some of his finest poems by the overuse of alliteration:

> For winter's rains and ruins are over,
> And all the season of snows and sins . . .

> O sweet stray sister, O shifting swallow,
> The heart's division divideth us . . .

In lines such as these, the alliteration becomes so heavy that the poem breaks down under the weight of sound. Swinburne himself recognized his failing and parodied it.

Yet more delicately employed, as in the *l* sounds in this passage from Tennyson, alliteration justifies the place it holds in our poetic history:

>   . . . ah, why
> Should *l*ife all *l*abour be?
> *L*et us a*l*one. Time driveth onward fast,
> And in a *l*ittle while our *l*ips are dumb.
> *L*et us a*l*one. What is it that will *l*ast?
> All things are taken from us, and become
> *P*ortions and *p*arcels of the dreadful *P*ast.

The *p* alliteration in the last line strikes us as being too heavy. There is not nearly so much of it as of the *l* sound; yet there is too much in close relation, whereas the *l* sounds are scattered.

Assonance

Assonance was the chief adornment of Old French poetry. It is a combination of similar vowel sounds. Though hitherto it has never had any set pattern in English verse, it is to-day being employed occasionally in place of rhyme by such modern poets as Archibald

MacLeish and W. H. Auden. Its normal function is to enrich a line, as in Waller's

Go, lovely Rose.

A careful examination of Coleridge's "Kubla Khan" will reveal a striking use of assonance throughout the poem, and, in the first line, an almost geometric pattern of similar vowel sounds:

"In Xan a du did Ku bla Khan."

Or consider the delicate play of assonance in Shakspere's line:

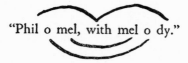

"Phil o mel, with mel o dy."

The danger of using assonance is that one might give the effect of false rhyme (see below). For example, the words *line* and *time* should not be used as assonance, because the consonant sounds are too close.

Rhyme

And so we come to one of the major problems of our verse: rhyme. Theoretically, there may be no artistic justification for this device, but in practice it has certainly proved to be one of the most natural ornaments of our poetry. Milton, whose rhymes are the least successful part of his poetic technique, said of rhyme: "It is no necessary adjunct or true ornament of poem or good verse . . . but the invention of a barbarous age to set off wretched matter and lame metre." Wilde, on the other hand, called it "the one string we have added to the Greek lyre." With this opinion, most of the poets, in their practice at any rate, seem to agree.

The first charge against rhyme is that it limits or changes the idea. There is only one answer to that: don't let it. Suppose you are working at top speed on some particularly felicitous poem. You are saying something, you are saying it musically—and then, suddenly you are brought face to face with what seems to be an insoluble rhyme-puzzle. The chances are that the puzzle is not insoluble. Try hard to solve it. Perhaps you are unsuccessful, and it seems that all the energy you were formerly devoting to your poem is now directed to the rhyme and being wasted. If such be the case, leave the rhyme unsolved and go on with your work. Finish the poem and put it away for a few days. Probably you will then find that the puzzle was not so hard as you thought, that the phrase you wished to cling to is not really so effective after all, that the line can be swung into your scheme by a change that is really for the better. I have just one reason for urging this suggestion: I have never known it to fail. Of course, you must sometimes be very bold, even heartless, in taking out phrases and whole lines, but that is as it should be. For all composition succeeds as much by omission as commission. The eraser is the one implement common to all the arts—and it is one of the most serviceable.

It may be that your rhyming will suggest an apt embellishment to your idea. That is one of the rewards of rhyming. But be very careful not to let your rhyme shift the main value of your poem. This danger accounts for my opposition to the use of a rhyming dictionary. When we go through the alphabet looking for rhyme words we seek those that will best fit what we wish to say, but if we open to a page on which all the rhyme words are displayed, immediately there starts up in our mind a train of as many ideas as there are words before us. We are entranced with the rhyming possibilities open to us, and before we know what we have done, we have entirely lost our original theme in favor of another, or several others, suggested by the words before us. And there is an end of the poem we intended. We have substituted for it some verses very cleverly rhymed, but probably possessing no other virtue. Indeed, rhyme is justified by this function if no other: it increases the difficulty of our medium, and spurs us on to our best efforts; it provides friction sufficient to heat our materials without burning them up. If we retain rhyme and at the same time remove its difficulty, we have merely an incentive to long-windedness. Therefore, I should advise against the use of a rhyming dictionary.

Not only must we not allow rhyme to falsify our idea; we must not allow it to wrench our words out of their natural order. The feeblest versifiers have always made inversions. And, it must be admitted, so have some of the best poets in the language. But we should not pattern ourselves after the weaker moments of our models. Inversions have become more and more repugnant to competent poets. When the reader finds us saying *meadows gay* instead of *gay meadows,* he knows perfectly well that we were forced to make the inversion in order to rhyme with *day* two lines above, and in this knowledge he is equipped to make fun of us. No artist must ever be found out when he is playing tricks—and rhyme is one of the hardest tricks in the language.

Remember, then, that rhyme is the last consideration of all. We must maintain our idea in its original values, we must maintain the music of our verse, we must maintain the natural prose order of our words. Without disturbing any of these elements, we must rhyme. That is the task which no one can perform for any one else. It can be done by the individual poet if he will practice long enough, if he is willing to face his work as seriously as the pianist learning his scales or the painter studying anatomy. The trouble with most writers of verse is that they are idle fellows who have turned to verse because they think it requires less hard labor than the other arts.

Rhyme is a very ancient device which probably had its origin in the Orient. It appeared in medieval Latin songs, then in Old French poetry, and, during the twelfth century, began to appear in England, where finally it vanquished alliteration as a set pattern. Rhyme is a combination of two or more words with the same terminal vowel and consonant sounds and differing initial consonant sounds. There are four kinds of rhyme:

1. Normal rhyme:

      sing   *spring*

   Or, in two-syllable endings:
   November   *remember*

2. Imperfect rhyme, in which we find a slight change in the vowel sound:

      love   *prove*

   Or, in two-syllable endings:
   temple   *simple*

Imperfect rhymes may be used sparingly to relieve the monotony of a set rhyme scheme. It is now stylish to overdo the effect of imperfect rhyme; avoid being stylish in this matter as in all others pertaining to art.

3. Identical rhyme, in which two words with different spelling, but the same sound, are combined:

      rain   *reign*

   Or, in two-syllable endings:
   wither   *whither*

Identical rhymes, though permitted in French, are not good form in English verse.

4. False rhyme, in which the terminal consonant is not the same:

      time   *line*

Or, in two-syllable rhyme:

tender   *remember*

This sort of rhyming is taboo.

Certain rhyming combinations are to be avoided because they are hackneyed and obvious. Of these I should list among the most common: *love–above, strife–life, breath–death, desire–fire, star–far, earth–birth, breeze–trees, heart–smart, together–heather, spring–sing.* These are a few out of a large category which should be familiar to every reader who has suffered from the perusal of amateur lyrics. Of course, it would be absurd to lay down a law against any of these combinations; we can only say that they have been too often and too loosely used, and that he is a powerful technician who can make them again effective.

The problem of imperfect rhymes has also troubled many a poet. Used sparingly, imperfect rhymes are sometimes pleasant. We have the traditional *love-prove* combination, and the long and short sounds of *i,* as in the couplet by Marvell:

> And yonder all before us lie
> Deserts of vast eternity.

There are many other slight variations of the vowel sound which are not unpleasant to the discerning ear as long as they are introduced very seldom.

We should also be careful in the manipulation of our "weak" endings. For example, *melody,* the last syllable of which is weak, should never be rhymed with another word with a weak ending, such as *liberty,* but with some strong syllable, such as *free,* which will hold up the rhyme sound competently. In like manner, we should not rhyme *loveliness* with *visionless,* since both endings are weak. Furthermore, in employing words with weak endings, even where they are coupled with strong endings, we must beware of "identical" rhyme sounds. Thus, we can not rhyme *visionless* with *less,* because we have simply repeated the same syllable, and that is forbidden. This law is well known to everybody, yet it is amazing how often it is violated. I have recently seen a poem in print where *sovereign* is rhymed with *rain,* and through sheer carelessness.

Random "internal" rhymes are also to be avoided. Thus, we should not write this couplet:

> Then to the bed they lifted up the dead
> The laurel crown still clinging to his head.

The word *bed* in the body of the line rings an extra bell, and destroys that nice order of repeated sound which is the sole justification for rhyme.

Turn back to that magnificent lyric by the late Poet Laureate, "The Evening Darkens Over" (on page 14). Note how skilfully he manipulates the two-syllable, or "feminine" rhymes. Note the distribution of alliteration and assonance, the complete polish of the whole, and the fine dramatic effect of the last line.

You have noticed, too, that most of the feminine rhymes are imperfect? And that a single rhyme sound pervades all the masculine rhymes of the poem? That the diction is absolutely simple and pictorial? Then I am making myself understood.

CHAPTER 3

METRE

FOR convenience, we classify the various kinds of English metre according to the arrangement of stress, or accent, which is the predominant characteristic of our verse. We speak of five-stress lines (pentameter), four-stress lines (tetrameter), and qualify these terms by taking into account the position of the weak, or unstressed syllables, as well. Thus, a foot consisting of one weak syllable followed by an accented syllable we call an iamb; and five of these constitute an iambic pentameter, four of them an iambic tetrameter, and so forth. Terminology in itself has no importance, and many writers, discarding the old terms, speak of an iambic pentameter as a five-stress iambic line and of an iambic tetrameter as a four-stress iambic line. Since this practice seems the simpler, we shall adopt it here.

Though readers are doubtless familiar with the names of the most important feet in verse, it might be well to give examples of them here, so that we may use the terms as a sort of shorthand code in analyzing the various metrical patterns which we shall discuss.

The two-part metres are the iambic and trochaic.

The iambic foot consists of a weak syllable followed by a strong: *de light'*. The trochaic foot consists of a strong syllable followed by a weak: *splen' did*. The three-part metres are the dactyl, the amphibrach, and the anapest, with the stresses arranged thus: dactyl, *ten' der ly;* amphibrach, *de light' ful;* and anapest, *in ter twine'*. According to this terminology, we should call this line,

> And away' in the east' we disco'vered our home',

a four-stress anapestic; or this one,

> Call' no more' across' the si'lent wa'ter,

a five-stress trochaic line.

The four-syllable feet are called paeons, and are of especial interest. There are four kinds of paeons, each determined by the placing of the accent within the foot. In the First paeon, the accent is on the first syllable, as in the opening of Masefield's famous "Cargoes": "Quinquereme of / Nineveh from / distant Ophir." The Second paeon can be illustrated with a folk rhyme: "The King was in / his counting house." The Third paeon serves as a basis for the opening of De la Mare's "Listeners": "Is there any / body there / said the Traveler." The Fourth paeon is seldom encountered: "There is a hand / whiter than pearl," but it is interesting to note that the famous V for Victory rhythm, which is also the rhythm of a theme from Beethoven's Fifth Symphony, is a Fourth paeon.

As in the case of the three-syllable feet, these four-syllable feet are most usually found without their full

quota of syllables, pauses and long vowel sounds fre-
quently making up for the missing syllables. Note, for
example, the three-syllable foot "body there" in the
example from "The Listeners" quoted above. It is easy
to shift from one kind of paeon to another, and two or
three paeonic rhythms may be found in the same poem.
Furthermore, they easily shift back into two-syllable
verse. The reason for this is simple: The first and third
paeons consist of two trochaic feet with one accent
muted; the second and fourth paeons consist of two
iambic feet with one accent muted.

Paeonic verse is closely related to the old accentual
freedom of Anglo-Saxon versification. It is found in
folk poetry, nursery rhymes, and in modern usage
where an effect of simplicity and strength is desired.
Gerard Manley Hopkins averred that his versification
was based on the First paeon: take, for example, the first
line of his sonnet, "Spring": "Nothing is so beautiful
as spring."

Let us simplify matters at once by limiting our dis-
cussion to the iambic measure in its various forms.
There is good reason for such limitation. The iamb
is the natural metre of English verse, and until we have
mastered this metre, we had best not venture into the
less natural, and therefore more difficult, rhythms. Fur-
thermore, if we master this metre thoroughly, we shall
find ourselves well equipped to employ the trochaic
and the three-part measures which, although for some
strange reason they always attract the novice, are all

too apt to become monotonous. Pure trochaic verse gives an effect of hammering monotony; the pure three-part measures fall into a monotonous lilt. Even iambic verse, though not to the same degree as the others, becomes monotonous if we do not vary it with frequent irregularities. We may, therefore, narrow our discussion even further, to the consideration of just how much, and in what manner, we should vary our verse to prevent monotony.

Here is a perfectly regular five-stress iambic line:

In sooth', I know' not why' I am' so sad'.

Thus Shakspere opens *The Merchant of Venice,* illustrating, by the way, an important metrical principle. Let your first line, or even your opening passage, be as nearly regular as possible, to establish the normal metre in the reader's ear. Then, through your whole poem, if you vary skilfully, without roughness, the reader will always be aware of two rhythms subtly supporting and relieving each other: the normal iambic rhythm basically, and over that, the play of well modulated variations. One critic has compared the music of English verse to Chopin's playing—his left hand keeping absolute tempo, his right hand weaving over that tempo a rich assortment of secondary rhythms. The natural ear of the poet comes into play in determining just how much variation he may introduce without roughening his metre.

The most important of recognized irregularities in iambic verse are as follows:

The trisyllabic foot:

> What man' ner of man' are you' my lord' I said'.

The second foot, it will be noted, contains three, instead of the normal two, syllables—an effective variation because neither of the unaccented syllables is too heavy. Had the line been written thus,

> Who then', rash old man' are you' my lord' I said',

the trisyllabic foot would have been unendurably awkward, and would have completely upset the balanced rhythm of the line.

The feminine ending:

> And down' the hill' we walked' toge'ther.

Here, it will be noted, the last foot has an extra weak syllable, a "feminine," or double, ending. Used sparingly, this device is agreeable; used too freely, it brings a rather jog-trot rhythm into the verse. Remember that in rhyming a feminine ending, both syllables must enter into the rhyme, not merely the last one. For example, we could rhyme *together* with *feather,* but never with *stir,* which is a single, or "masculine" ending. In verse, the two sexes stand obstinately apart.

The transferred accent:

> Spurn' ing the lad' der of' their late' as cent'.

In the initial foot, the accent has been transferred from its normal place to the first syllable of the foot. We sometimes find the same device in the body of the line, as here in the third foot:

> When fell′ the dark′ bring′ ing its bea′ con stars′.

This device is the commonest of metrical variations, and so natural that it may sometimes be introduced even into the opening line of a poem without disturbing the normal rhythm, as in Keats's famous sonnet on Chapman's Homer:

> Much′ have I trav′ell'd in′ the realms′ of gold′.

The Spondee:

In classical verse the two long syllables within the single foot are an intrinsic part of metrical pattern. In English, the spondee consists of two accented syllables within the single foot and is so rare that it is a variation rather than a basic metrical unit. The difficulty of fashioning graceful spondees in English constitutes one of the main obstacles in the approximation of classical effects in our language.

> The horsemen rode *bright-shod* with flying sparks

The third foot consists of two accented syllables. Skilfully used, so as to avoid heaviness, the spondee is a welcome variation.

Hovering accent:

> The rude′ foréfa′ thers of′ the ham′ let sleep′.

This line illustrates one of the most delicate and pleasing of metrical variations. In the second foot, neither

the first nor the second syllable receives a full stress;
they are of equal accent and share the stress of the foot
between them. At its best, this hovering accent gives a
delightful undulation to the line.

Perhaps the reader will already have noticed that in
the two lines last quoted, a full stress falls on a weak
preposition. We have scanned the line from Gray's
Elegy so that in the third foot the stress falls on the
word *of,* yet obviously we should not accent this word
heavily in reading the poem aloud. It is clear that our
theoretical scansion and our actual rendering of the
poem have parted company. Right here the whole
theory of English verse, as stressed verse merely, breaks
down. We therefore look for another element in our
rhythm to account for this phenomenon, and we find
it in the *tempo* of the verse, the *time element,* which is
almost as important as the accentual element, and per-
haps even more important as a means toward varying
our metre skilfully. Let us take the famous lyric from
The Tempest, and scan it according to strict accentual
convention:

1. Full fath' om five' thy fa' ther lies';
2. Of' his bones' are cor' al made',
3. Those' are pearls' that were' his eyes':
4. No' thing of' him that' doth fade',
5. But' doth suf' fer a' sea-change'
6. In' to some' thing rich' and strange'.
7. Sea'-nymphs hour' ly ring' his knell':
8. Ding'-dong'.

9. Hark! now' I hear' them—
10. Ding'-dong', bell'!

For the most part, these lines are "beheaded" iambic lines—or iambic lines with the initial weak syllable omitted. Yet, most decidedly, we do not read the poem as we have scanned it. The time element controls much of the poem more strongly than the accentual element. In line 1, the long *i* sounds break the line into two halves; in 2, the long *o* of *bones,* and the long *a* of *made,* follow suit; *pearls* and *eyes* divide the next line; line 4 goes back into accentual rhythm; 5 again breaks into two parts and is further slowed up considerably by the hovering accent of *sea-change* (here so heavy as to constitute a *spondee*); 6 is again largely accentual, as is 7. Line 8 is perhaps the most interesting of all. The Elizabethans were apt to take their dramatists literally. If, in a play, a character remarks that he hears the cock crowing, there will be the sound of the cock crow off-stage. And probably, when the singer had pronounced the syllable *ding* in line 8, he paused while a bell was rung, and again after the syllable *dong.* Note that if we include the two bell notes we have, in duration of time, as long a line here as elsewhere, thus: Ding (bell) Dong (bell). It is significant that Ariel, in line 9 of the poem remarks: *Now I hear them.*

To summarize, then, the time-element in English metre is not fixed, but is another variation woven over the accentual metre. Its contributions to the music of

verse are the pause (called the *cæsura*) and the hasten-
ing or slackening of metre by the time-length of vari-
ous syllables. Let us rescan this poem according to the
double standard of time and stress:

> Full fathom *five* / thy father *lies;* /
> Of his *bones* / are coral *made,* /
> Those are *pearls* / that were his *eyes:* /
> No'thing of' him that' doth fade', /
> But' doth suf'fer / a *sea'-change'* /
> Into' some'thing rich' and strange'. /
> *Sea'-nymphs'* hour'ly ring' his knell': /
> *Ding (bell)* / *dong (bell)* /
> Hark! now' I hear' them— /
> *Ding' dong'*, bell'! /

I have not introduced this rather elaborate theory
merely for its own sake, but for the understanding of
certain principles which must control our practice, and
may as well control it intelligently.

The lesson we learn from considering the time ele-
ment in verse, then, is that the best expression of our
mood or idea may sometimes depend on the subtle vari-
ations of pause and syllabic time-value. Consider the
arrangements of the pause in this stanza by Ben Jonson:

> Still to be neat, / still to be drest, /
> As you were going to a feast; /
> Still to be powder'd, / still perfumed: /
> Lady, / it is to be presumed, /
> Though art's hid causes are not found, /
> All is not sweet, / all is not sound. /

Consider the difference in tempo between these two lines, both of which are five-stress iambics according to our accentual scansion:

> And ten low words oft creep in one dull line

and

> Wake! for the sun has scattered into flight

We may hurry our metre by omitting the pause, not only within the line, but even between one line and the next or through a whole passage; we may slacken it by introducing frequent pauses. Syllabically, we may make haste with a swift word such as *scattering,* or hold up our tempo by such a spondaic combination as *strength well won,* which, of the same stress value theoretically as *scattering,* nevertheless is very much slower and more ponderous. The main care must be to adapt our tempo to what we are expressing.

CHAPTER 4

BASIC METRICAL FORMS

THE four-stress couplet is the oldest rhymed form in the language. A poem of the early thirteenth century, Lay-amon's *Brut,* is an interesting combination of the alliterative style that was going out and the rhymed couplet which supplanted it. The possibilities and limitations of the form are sharply defined by centuries of experiment.

In the first place, the form will test to the full your ability to vary musically, for no measure falls into monotony more readily. The line-length is essentially lyric; indeed, the larger proportion of our lyric literature is based on four-stress metre. Like the Anglo-Saxon line which it supplanted, the four-stress line will accept great syllabic irregularity, but in spite of that it lapses into monotony in the course of a long poem. Milton's "L'Allegro" and "Il Penseroso" are the longest successful poems in four-stress couplets, and it would be folly for a beginner to attempt poems even as long as these. The history of English poetry is strewn with examples of long failures in this form from Chaucer to Masefield.

Let us take two stanzas from Christopher Marlowe:

Come live with me and be my Love,
And we will all the pleasures prove
That hills and valleys, dales and fields,
Or woods or steepy mountain yields. . . .

And I will make thee beds of roses
And a thousand fragrant posies;
A cap of flowers, and a kirtle
Embroider'd all with leaves of myrtle.

In this lyric, Marlowe, whose genius for subtle variation is almost unsurpassed, has kept fairly close to the normal metre, yet we notice at once the variety in the placing of the pauses, and, in the second stanza, the "feminine" or two-syllable endings to the line. Furthermore, we find that the second line in the second stanza is not iambic at all, but trochaic. The line scans thus:

And a thóu sand ffa grant pós ies

The introductory weak syllable of the normal iambic foot has been omitted. This omission is important, for it constitutes one of the main differences between four- and five-stress iambic measure. The omission of the introductory weak syllable in a passage of five-stress iambic verse is nearly always awkward and jarring and should be avoided; in four-stress iambic metre, this "beheading" of the line is one of the most common and necessary variations.

If you examine "L'Allegro" carefully, you will discover that about a third of the lines are thus beheaded. Sometimes you find complete paragraphs of such lines:

Streit mine eye hath caught new pleasures
Whilst the Landskip round it measures,
Russet Lawns, and Fallows Gray,
Where the nibbling flocks do stray,
Mountains on whose barren brest
The labouring clouds do often rest.

The final line of this passage restores the weak syllable at the beginning (and note the three syllables in the second foot); the rest are all beheaded. The effect intended, of course, is one of swiftness and lightness. In "Il Penseroso" the proportion of beheaded lines is much smaller. Milton's prosodic problem in sustaining and varying the mood in these two poems is more complicated than any you are likely to face at this stage of your experience, hence his variations are bolder and more frequent than yours will need to be.

Finally, for the freest treatment of this form, read and study Coleridge's "Christabel." Here the poet has fallen back on the time element in our verse. We find lines in "Christabel" like the two-syllable line from Shakspere's lyric quoted earlier (page 39) in which we can not possibly hear four stresses. The explanation is that these lines, though syllabically deficient, are equal in time to the others if we extend the duration of the words and mark the pauses or "rests." We also discover a constantly shifting movement of the verse to conform to the movement of the narrative. Frequently these modulations take the form of long passages in three-part metre (anapests and dactyls).

For the beginner, however, it would be wiser to hold more closely to the normal measure, particularly in a short lyric. Andrew Marvell's "To His Coy Mistress" is an excellent example of the four-stress couplet varied in exact propriety to the needs of the occasion. A short quotation will suffice:

> . . . But at my back I always hear
> Time's wingëd chariot hurrying near;
> And yonder all before us lie
> Deserts of vast eternity.
> Thy beauty shall no more be found,
> Nor, in thy marble vault, shall sound
> My echoing song: then worms shall try
> That long preserved virginity,
> And your quaint honour turn to dust,
> And into ashes all my lust:
> The grave's a fine and private place,
> But none, I think, do there embrace.

Note how the syntax of the sentence runs without break from line 3 into line 4, line 6 into line 7, and line 7 into line 8. This device of pushing the rhythm of one line into the next is known as *enjambment* or *run-over,* and is found frequently throughout English poetry—and Classical poetry as well. (See the chapter "On Reading Verse Aloud.")

The next step in the study of rhyme is a consideration of the four-stress quatrain with alternating rhymes: *a b a b.* This is a rather slow-paced lyric measure, in general, and is common throughout our poetry. A stanza of George Herbert's "Easter" will serve as an example:

I got me flowers to straw Thy way,
   I got me boughs off many a tree;
But Thou wast up by break of day,
   And brought'st Thy sweets along with Thee.

More important is the quatrain in alternating line-lengths of four- and three-stress measure. This is known as ballad metre and is originally found in some of the oldest folk-ballads and songs in the language. In its original form, the rhyme scheme was usually *a b c b,* leaving the first and third lines unrhymed. Such rhyming is still appropriate when a poet wishes to capture the mood of the old ballad, an archaic effect such as is found in parts of Coleridge's "Ancient Mariner":

(4-stress)	The Sun now rose upon the right:	(a)
(3-stress)	Out of the sea came he,	(b)
(4-stress)	Still hid in mist, and on the left	(c)
(3-stress)	Went down into the sea.	(b)

Unless we desire to imitate the old ballad, it is best to avoid the rhyme-scheme which leaves lines one and three unrhymed. Ballad metre rhyming *a b a b* is demanded when this stanza is used for formal lyric composition, as in Herrick's

     Bid me to live, and I will live
       Thy Protestant to be;
     Or bid me love, and I will give
       A loving heart to thee.

Judging from the practice of reputable poets, we may say that the "lazy" rhyme-scheme, *a b c b* is never used except in the imitation of folk-ballad. In five-stress quatrains it would be barbarous. The general doctrine in rhymed verse is to rhyme everything. Conversely, in blank verse or unrhymed verse in general, there should be no rhyme at all. In short, rhyme everything or nothing.

The "In Memoriam" stanza, as its name indicates, is inescapably bound up with Tennyson's great elegy. Like the "Omar Khayyam" stanza, it is so associated with a single masterpiece that it has seldom been used elsewhere. The stanza is in four-stress lines rhymed *a b b a:*

> Love is and was my Lord and King,
>   And in his presence I attend
>   To hear the tidings of my friend
> Which every hour his couriers bring.
>
> Love is and was my King and Lord,
>   And will be, tho' as yet I keep
>   Within his court on earth, and sleep
> Encompass'd by his faithful guard,
>
> And hear at times a sentinel
>   Who moves about from place to place,
>   And whispers to the world of space,
> In the deep night, that all is well.

Turning to the five-stress quatrain, we find a dignified, rather slow-paced form rhymed *a b a b,* and known as the *heroic quatrain. Heroic,* as used in relation to the heroic quatrain and the heroic couplet, may be regarded as a synonym for *Classical* rather than indicating a treatment of heroic material. In 1599 Sir John Davies published his philosophical poem *Nosce Teipsum,* the first extended poem in heroic quatrains, from which anthologists delight to extract two out of the scores of stanzas, though there are many fine passages:

> I know my soul hath power to know all things,
> Yet she is blind and ignorant in all.
> I know I'm one of Nature's little kings,
> Yet to the least and vilest things am thrall.
>
> I know my life's a pain and but a span;
> I know my sense is mock'd in everything;
> And, to conclude, I know myself a Man—
> Which is a proud and yet a wretched thing.

The large majority of poets have used the heroic quatrain occasionally. The present Poet Laureate, John Masefield, has made it the vehicle for several important works, notably "August, 1914." Like most other poems in this grave stanza, "August, 1914" is in the elegiac mood best represented by the greatest of all poems in the heroic quatrain, Thomas Gray's "Elegy Written in a Country Churchyard." Lastly, it should be noted that the heroic quatrain is the main unit in the Shaksperian Sonnet, which, metrically, consists of three heroic quatrains followed by a heroic couplet.

The term *heroic couplet* is properly limited to that use of the *five-stress* couplet wherein each couplet is a separate unit and there is no enjambment from one couplet to another, but in common parlance the five-stress couplet in general is often called the heroic couplet.

This simple form was originally known as "Riding Rhyme." It was extensively used by Chaucer in the *Canterbury Tales,* found favor with the Elizabethans, and at the end of the seventeenth century, in its closed, or heroic, phase, became the essential medium of English verse. The reign of the heroic couplet, beginning with Waller and Dryden, continuing through the satires of Pope, and reaching a distinguished conclusion in the works of Johnson, Goldsmith, and George Crabbe, lasted well over a century. Even the Romantic poets, at the beginning of the nineteenth century, who revolted against the strict closed couplet of their predecessors, the Augustans, nevertheless did not abandon the five-stress couplet, which they used with great freedom and much enjambment.

The form is excellently adapted for the epigram, and we have countless examples of memorable single couplets like Robert Herrick's tribute to the Virgin Mary:

> To work a wonder God would have her shown
> At once a bud and yet a rose full blown.

Or Donne's couplet on Lady Herbert:

> No spring, nor summer beauty hath such grace
> As I have seen in one autumnal face.

Note how much meaning is packed into these brief epigrams. Not a syllable is wasted, not an adjective in-

troduced to fill out the metre. Such economy of phras-
ing, such simplicity of statement, captivates the reader
at once. Compression and brilliant turn of phrase char-
acterize the couplets of Dryden and Pope, and a begin-
ner could not do better than to study these masters and
try a few couplets in their manner.

Or consider Francis Quarles' epigram in two couplets:

> My soul, sit thou a patient looker-on,
> Judge not the play before the play is done:
> Her plot hath many changes; every day
> Speaks a new scene; the last act crowns the play.

You will notice in this poem the swift enjambment in
the second couplet and the variety of pauses contrasting
with the regular beat of the introductory couplet. An
analysis of even this short poem reveals a number of
subtle irregularities without which the verse would be
monotonous and flat-footed.

It is not necessary, of course, to confine your experi-
ments to the epigram. The five-stress couplet is one of
the most flexible measures and may be adapted to al-
most any mood or theme. It has served our poets chiefly
as the vehicle for narrative, as in the works of Chaucer,
for satire, as in Pope, and even for pastoral poetry. Its
possibilities are unlimited. In his long poem, "King
Cole," for instance, Masefield used the five-stress couplet
for his dialogue, to set it off from the narrative, which
is in a seven-line five-stress stanza called "rime royal"
(having been a favorite form with King James I of
Scotland). And in Keats' "I stood tip-toe upon a little

hill," we find a free treatment of the form, flowing and well modulated, to communicate a mood inspired by natural beauty:

> I stood tip-toe upon a little hill,
> The air was cooling, and so very still,
> That the sweet buds which with a modest pride
> Pull droopingly, in slanting curve aside,
> Their scantly leav'd and finely tapering stems,
> Had not yet lost their starry diadems
> Caught from the early sobbing of the morn.
> The clouds were pure and white as flocks new shorn,
> And fresh from the clear brook; sweetly they slept
> On the blue fields of heaven, and then there crept
> A little noiseless noise among the leaves
> Born of the very sigh that silence heaves.

It may be that in attempting some such effect as this, you will find your verse becoming too loose, the lines not merely flowing into each other but slopping over. In that case, read Pope as a corrective. Pope constructs each couplet separately as a "thought-coop," a finished epigram in itself, almost without syllabic irregularity. The poem as a whole is bound together by the continuity of thought like the thread on which the single beads are strung. Many of Pope's single couplets have become proverbs and justly so. Read his "Esssay on Criticism" and "Epistle to Doctor Arbuthnot," and you will be struck by the familiarity of many of the sayings. As the lady said to her friend at a performance of King Lear, "My, this play is just full of proverbs, isn't it."

Gray's "Elegy" probably holds the record number in proportion to its length.

There are several stanza forms in five-stress verse which are standard. Most of them may be found in Chaucer, whose work is unsurpassed in variety and polish. There is the six-line stanza, for example, rhyming *a b a b c c.* (This is also the sestet of the Shaksperian sonnet.) Shakspere's "Venus and Adonis" is in this form. His "Rape of Lucrece" is in the much more important Rime Royal, a pattern still popular to this day, notably in the works of Masefield who has often used it for narrative, most effectively in his "Dauber." Rime Royal is a seven-line stanza rhyming *a b a b b c c.* The Elizabethans were especially fond of it, and scarcely a poet of the time neglected to employ it.

The Omar Khayyam quatrain, rhyming *a a b a,* is, as has been noted, too closely identified with FitzGerald's poem to recommend it for general use.

The "Monk's Tale" in the *Canterbury Tales* is composed in an eight-line stanza with a linked rhyme scheme, *a b a b b c b c.* Edmund Spenser, the great Chaucerian of his age, added a six-foot line (called an "Alexandrine") to the "Monk's Tale" stanza and thus created the Spenserian stanza, the vehicle of Spenser's *Faerie Queene,* Byron's *Childe Harold,* Keats' *Eve of St. Agnes,* Shelley's *Adonais* and many other works of major intention.

The Spenserian stanza has room for sufficient variation; it is not a form which invites monotony, but it is difficult and majestic, somewhat akin to the mood of Handel's music. As far as I know, no poet is using it today or has shown any especial sympathy for it. Perhaps the age is too nervous and rapid to enjoy the solemn Alexandrine concluding each stanza with a retarded gravity, a long line which subtly divides into two sections of three stresses each. (See the chapter "On Reading Verse Aloud.") As examples, we shall take two of the loftiest stanzas from "Adonais"; the *Faerie Queene,* being a narrative, does not so easily present single passages for selection:

> The splendours of the firmament of time
> May be eclipsed but are extinguish'd not;
> Like stars to their appointed height they climb,
> And death is a low mist which can not blot
> The brightness it may veil. When lofty thought
> Lifts a young heart above its mortal lair,
> And love and life contend in it for what
> Shall be its earthly doom, the dead live there,
> And move like winds of light on dark and stormy air.

> . . . The One remains; the many change and pass;
> Heaven's light for ever shines; earth's shadows fly;
> Life, like a dome of many-coloured glass,
> Stains the white radiance of eternity,
> Until Death tramples it to fragments.—Die,
> If thou wouldst be with that which thou dost seek!
> Follow where all is fled!—Rome's azure sky,
> Flowers, ruins, statues, music, words, are weak
> The glory they transfuse with fitting truth to speak.

Incidentally, the awkward and unacceptable inversion of syntax in the last line quoted is an example of what you should *not* do.

There are scores of other common stanza forms, and every poet will take delight in his own ingenuity in the arrangement of line-lengths and rhyme-schemes in recurrent patterns. Note the word *recurrent,* however. All verse is based on recurrence: the foot is the smallest unit of recurrence, the line comes next, and finally the stanza. In every stanza the rhymes must be in the same corresponding places: if the first one, for example, has the rhyme scheme *a b c b d c d,* all the stanzas following must follow the same arrangement. The rhyme sounds, however, should be clearly different. If in one stanza, the words *long* and *song* are used as rhymes, be sure that the same rhyme sound does not appear in the next one. The necessity of corresponding similarity exists between stanzas where lines are of unequal length. If in the first stanza the first line has three stresses, the second five, the third three, and the fourth six, so in all the following stanzas the first line must have three stresses, the second five, the third three, the fourth six, and so on.

In the first edition of this book, published some ten years ago, I advised practising with unrhymed verse before attempting rhymed verse. I have reversed that opinion. It seems best, since rhyme has become an integral part of our verbal music, to start out with it and let your technique follow the various forms in the same order in which they developed in the history of our verse. Unrhymed verse, furthermore, though easy to write, is hard to write well. The late Professor Shaler of Harvard, who was a geologist, took up verse as a hobby and declared that blank verse was easier to write than prose. He proved it by composing an extremely lengthy play in blank verse on the life of Queen Elizabeth which showed an admirable appreciation of that great sovereign but was almost unreadable.

The term "blank" verse is applied only to unrhymed verse in iambic pentameter. No form demands more caution against prolixity and looseness. It should not be attempted by the beginner. There are few principles beyond metrical rules that can be set down in relation to blank verse; it can only be developed by an exquisitely fine natural ear which has scrupulously listened to the work of the masters and is competent to add, within the rules, some new music of its own. It is best for the novice to compose in rhymed stanzas and couplets.

CHAPTER 5

THE SONNET

A PERUSAL of the rather slipshod sonnets now appearing in our magazines might convince us that the sonnet is merely an arbitrary form of fourteen lines and a certain rhyme scheme. The novice or the careless craftsman is too apt to preoccupy himself with the external form of the sonnet; he finds an idea, gropes for a certain number of words which rhyme, and then attempts to force the two elements together.

As a matter of fact, the sonnet is not an arbitrary form, but the result of a gradual and natural evolution. Nowhere in the history of versification is there a clearer example of the survival of the fittest than in this fourteen-line poem, the thought divisions of which are even more important than the rhyme-scheme. Hundreds of experiments in Italian, French, and English went into the shaping of this form. At its best, it is one of the most convenient and effective mediums which we possess for the expression of a single thought or emotion.

Although in English we have two major, and several minor, schemes for the sonnet, the underlying impulse for each is the same. We must have in mind a single theme which will adapt itself readily to (1) a simple statement, (2) a variation on that theme by metaphor, contrast, or comparison, (3) a secondary variation clearly subordinated to the first, and (4) either a re-statement with the effect of a climax or an anticipation of the main idea. In every good sonnet these elements will be found, though the order in which they are in-troduced varies widely. A frequent arrangement is to open the sonnet with the metaphor, and introduce the statement as an emphatic afterthought. In all cases, however, it is likely that the elements will be distributed through the fourteen lines of the sonnet in such man-ner that the *octave,* or first eight lines, will express the idea and the first variation, and the last six lines, called the *sestet,* will express the second variation and the cli-mactic restatement. So distinctive is this underlying thought-form that "sonnets" have been written in blank verse, without any rhymes at all (by Spenser and Keats), which are clearly recognizable as sonnets.

The *Shaksperian* or *English* Sonnet. The early Eng-lish sonneteers had difficulty in following the pure Ital-ian form,—which allows only two rhyme sounds in the octave,—because our language has far fewer similar rhyme sounds than the Italian. Therefore, they evolved a somewhat simpler form, known as the English sonnet, or, in honor of its greatest exponent, the Shaksperian sonnet. The two finest Elizabethan sonnet sequences, those of Shakspere and Michael Drayton, employ this

form. It consists of three heroic quatrains and a termi-
nal heroic couplet. The ideal thought-form for this
sonnet would fall into these divisions: first quatrain,
statement of the idea; second quatrain, metaphorical
variation on the idea; third quatrain, secondary vari-
ation on the idea; couplet, an epigrammatic summing
up. Note that in all sonnets, of whatever tradition, the
last line or the terminal couplet should present a mem-
orable summary of the thought, couched in as impres-
sive and sonorous diction as the poet can command.
The following sonnet of Michael Drayton's (from his
Idea) is generally considered a perfect example of the
Shaksperian form:

1

Since there's no help, come let us kiss and part—
Nay, I have done, you get no more of me;
And I am glad, yea, glad with all my heart,
That thus so cleanly I myself can free.

2

Shake hands for ever, cancel all our vows,
And when we meet at any time again,
Be it not seen in either of our brows
That we one jot of former love retain.

3

Now at the last gasp of Love's latest breath,
When, his pulse failing, Passion speechless lies,
When Faith is kneeling by his bed of death,
And Innocence is closing up his eyes,

4

—Now if thou would'st when all have given him over,
From death to life thou might'st him yet recover.

This sonnet, of course, should be printed as a single unit, without division. I have broken it up for the convenience of the reader. The octave consists of two quatrains closely allied in thought, the first expressing the main idea of farewell, and the second developing the idea of finality. The sestet opens with a radical change in the development of the idea. We have a quatrain in which the ministers of Love, the various attributes personified, witness the parting which has been expressed at the beginning of the sonnet. Then the couplet rises to a very fine climax by twisting the main idea of farewell to an unexpected angle. For the sake of emphasis, the elements have been arranged thus: (1) statement of the idea, (2) secondary variation on the idea, (3) primary variation on the idea through personification, (4) dramatic climax.

In many of Shakspere's sonnets, the statement of the main idea is withheld until the final couplet, where it is emphasized even more strongly by being combined with the emotional climax of the poem. This scheme results in the anticipation of the main idea by its primary and secondary development. Thus:

Shall I compare thee to a Summer's day?
Thou art more lovely and more temperate:
Rough winds do shake the darling buds of May,

And Summer's lease hath all too short a date:
Sometimes too hot the eye of heaven shines,
And often is his gold complexion dimm'd;
And every fair from fair sometime declines,
By chance or nature's changing course untrimm'd:
But thy eternal Summer shall not fade
Nor lose possession of that fair thou owest;
Nor shall Death brag thou wanderest in his shade,
When in eternal lines to time thou growest:
So long as men can breathe, or eyes can see,
So long lives this, and this gives life to thee.

The main idea of this sonnet, one of the commonest in all literature, is that the poet is eternalizing his beloved in his verse. We find the statement, combined with the emotional climax of the poem, in the couplet. The anticipation of the main idea we find at the beginning of the sestet: "But thy eternal Summer shall not fade." The primary development of the idea we find in the very first quatrain of the sonnet, and the secondary development in the second quatrain. This arrangement is a common one in Shakspere's sequence.

Let us now compare Shakspere's "Farewell" sonnet with Drayton's:

Farewell! thou art too dear for my possessing,
And like enough thou know'st thy estimate:
The charter of thy worth gives thee releasing;
My bonds in thee are all determinate.
For how do I hold thee but by thy granting?
And for that riches where is my deserving?
The cause of this fair gift in me is wanting,
And so my patent back again is swerving.

Thyself thou gav'st, thy own worth then not knowing,
Or me, to whom thou gav'st it, else mistaking;
So thy great gift, upon misprision growing,
Comes home again, on better judgment making.
Thus have I had thee, as a dream doth flatter
In sleep a King; but waking, no such matter.

In this sonnet, the four elements of the thought-form
are arranged in their simplest order: first quatrain, the
statement of the main idea; second quatrain, the pri-
mary variation; first quatrain of the sestet, the secondary
variation; and couplet, a restatement of the idea.

The *Petrarchan,* or *Italian,* Sonnet. The underlying
scheme of this sonnet must include the same four ele-
ments which we found in the Shaksperian sonnet,
though their distribution differs slightly. Whereas the
Shaksperian sonnet tends to fall into four parts,—the
three quatrains and the terminal couplet,—the Petrar-
chan is more distinctly two parts, the octave and the
sestet, though there are divisions in each of these main
parts. The rhyme scheme of the octave is fixed, and will
permit no liberties: *a b b a a b b a.* As a rule, there is
a division, or at least a pause or break in sentence
structure, between the first four and second four lines of
the octave. The last six lines of the Petrarchan sonnet
present a more complicated problem, because several
divisions of the thought are permissible, and, in con-
sequence, several different rhyme schemes. The two
most common arrangements of the rhymes are *c d e c*

d e, and *c d c d c d.* The first of these schemes will
follow a thought form which breaks evenly into two
divisions. Our sestet will then consist of two tercets
with a break between them, each rhymed *c d e.* The
other rhyme scheme, *c d c d c d,* may also break into
two tercets, or the break may come after the first four
lines (this arrangement being probably the result of
the Shaksperian sonnet), or even after the first five
lines, leaving the terminal line in isolated grandeur
with the effect of tremendous emphasis. Note that
all Petrarchan sonnets should conclude with a single
line as impressive and memorable as possible. Consider
these terminal lines from some of our best Petrarchan
sonnets:

Silent, upon a peak in Darien.

Keats.

The army of unalterable law.

Meredith.

The surge and thunder of the Odyssey.

Lang.

Despair before us, vanity behind.

Santayana.

There are various other rhyme schemes for the Petrar-
chan sestet, some of the commonest of which are: *c d c
d d c*; *c d c e d e*; *c d e d e c*; *c d e d c e.* The thought
divisions in these schemes will fall almost anywhere for
the most effective presentation of the idea, but, in gen-
eral, it is well to preserve a fairly even balance and never

to permit the final division to overbalance the one be-
fore it.

Let us divide Meredith's "Lucifer in Starlight" ac-
cording to the development of thought:

Octave (I) Primary variation.	On a starred night Prince Lucifer up- rose. Tired of his dark dominion swung the fiend Above the rolling ball in cloud part screened Where sinners hugged their spectre of repose.
(II) Secondary variation.	Poor prey to his hot fit of pride were those. And now upon his western wing he leaned, Now his huge bulk o'er Afric's sands careened, Now the black planet shadowed Arctic snows.
Sestet (I) Anticipation of Main Idea.	Soaring through wider zones that pricked his scars With memory of the old revolt from Awe, He reached a middle height, and at the stars, Which are the brain of heaven, he looked, and sank.
(II) Climax and Main Idea.	Around the ancient track marched, rank on rank, The army of unalterable law.

As a matter of fact, we should find it difficult to discover in English poetry many examples of the pure Petrarchan sonnet. D. G. Rossetti, in his "House of Life" sequence, is the most faithful of our Petrarchan sonneteers, but even he takes a good many liberties. In spite of the protests of purists, a compromise form has developed in English poetry which combines with the Petrarchan octave a Shaksperian sestet. The objection to this form is only theoretical; in practice, the form is one of the finest. George Santayana's noble sequence employs this mode extensively, and we could not find a better example of it than this sonnet of his:

As in the midst of battle there is room
For thoughts of love, and in foul sin for mirth;
As gossips whisper of a trinket's worth
Spied by the deathbed's flickering candle-gloom;
As in the crevices of Caesar's tomb
The sweet herbs flourish on a little earth,
So in this great disaster of our birth,
We may be happy and forget our doom.

For morning, with a ray of tenderest joy,
Gilding the iron heavens, hides the truth;
And evening gently woos us to employ
Our grief in idle catches. Such is youth,
Till from that summer's trance we wake, to find
Despair before us, vanity behind.

Incidentally, for a study of the modern Petrarchan sonnet, we could not find a better model than Santayana's sequence.

Of the minor forms of the sonnet, the best, though

the most neglected, is the Spenserian. This form, with its interlocking rhyme scheme, is particularly sonorous and fluent. Why later poets have avoided it so consistently is one of the mysteries of our verse. Its thought-form is the same as that of the Shaksperian sonnet, though its rhyme scheme is as follows: *a b a b b c b c c d c d e e:*

> Most glorious Lord of Life! that, on this day,
> Didst make Thy triumph over death and sin;
> And, having harrowed hell, didst bring away
> Captivity thence captive, us to win:
> This joyous day, dear Lord, with joy begin;
> And grant that we, for whom Thou diddest die,
> Being with Thy dear blood clean washed from sin,
> May live for ever in felicity!
> And that Thy love, we weighing worthily,
> May likewise love Thee for the same again;
> And for Thy sake, which all like dead didst buy,
> With love may one another entertain!
> So let us love, dear Love, like as we ought,
> Love is the lesson which the Lord us taught.

The study of the sonnet will bring to your attention a hundred details and permissible variations for which we have not space in these pages. Yet a few general rules may be appropriate:

(1) Remember that the sonnet is not a tyrant, but a benevolent despot elected, after hundreds of experiments, by the unanimous vote of the poets. If you do not mean to keep its laws, do not enter its territory.

(2) Remember that the inner shape of the thought is more important than the matter of rhymes.

(3) Be as fluent and natural as you can, that the form may not seem to cramp your thought or obtrude itself.

(4) Let no part of the sonnet be conspicuously out of tone with the rest. Sonnets which are "written around" a single phrase or line are always padded and weak.

(5) Do not indulge in violent irregularities of metre, for the sonnet is not long enough to sustain much variation from the norm.

(6) Never "behead" the lines of a sonnet.

(7) Rhyme as inconspicuously as possible.

(8) And again, *think* in sonnet form before writing a sonnet.

(9) Begin with the Shaksperian form.

(10) Finally, beware lest you fall into the "sonnet habit." If you have written so many sonnets that your thoughts arrive in no other form, eschew the sonnet until your technique has recovered its balance. The perennial sonneteer is one of the familiar victims of prosody.

CHAPTER 6

SOME FRENCH FORMS

THOUGH the so-called French forms are in no wise essential to our verse, they exercise a certain charm, and the practice of them can not fail to add to our facility. We have not, in English, many fine poems in these forms; success in them is rare. For one thing, we have not so many rhymes in English as there are in French, nor do we permit, as the French do, an identical rhyme, or repetition of the same rhyme sound in a different sense.

Dante boasted that the exigencies of his form, *terza rima,* never forced him to alter the sense of what he had to say. Yet, except for Shelley's "Ode to the West Wind" and Bridges' "London Snow," our language can not show a great poem in *terza rima,* because we have not the abundance of similar rhyme sounds, necessary to this form, which Italian yields to the poet. Thus, every language has its opportunities and limitations which determine the conventions of its versification. The classic French alexandrine, with the medial cæsura, is not effective in English; our blank verse falls dully on the Gallic ear. Such forms as the ballade (be

careful not to confuse this with the ordinary ballad)
or the rondeau are adaptable to the needs of English
poetry, but never seem quite so comfortable with us as
in their original home. They tend to force our poets
into prettiness or verbiage.

No artist can afford to alter the sense of what he has
to say in order to conform to his medium. Thus, al-
though we should cultivate difficult forms which stimu-
late by opposition the idea we have in mind, we should
not waste our time on forms the difficulty of which is
so great as to change, force, or limit our meaning. The
sonnet is safely on the side of good form—in every
sense of the phrase. The days of its naturalization are
so long past that it is hardly distinguishable from the
native subjects of the English muse. Although the
Petrarchan sonnet does present considerable difficulty,
we have so many and so conspicuous triumphs in this
mode that we may undoubtedly count it among our
most effective.

With the ballade we are on more debatable ground.
English has no poems in this manner to compare with
the ballades of François Villon. Graceful ballades we
have, and a few that are memorable, but the pattern
has not inspired our poets to their best efforts. Swin-
burne has written some good ones, but, more often
than not, he takes liberties with the form and fails
to carry the same rhyme sounds through the entire
poem. Rossetti's translations of Villon are faulty and
in no wise convey the splendour of the originals. Here

and there we chance on a ballade in English which is at once correct and significant, but a collection of such pieces would not fill a very large volume.

Though the ballade had many variations and was done to death even in France by too ingenious practitioners, the basic form has the following rhyme scheme: three stanzas built on three rhyme sounds, *a b a b b c b c,* (note the "Monk's Tale" stanza, p. 53) and an *envoi* (generally in the form of an apostrophe) rhyming *b c b c.* The final line, moreover, identical in all four divisions, constitutes a refrain. The problem is complicated. We must find fourteen different words to provide us with the *b* rhymes, six for the *a* rhymes, and eight for the *c* rhymes. Also, the refrain must always fall into place naturally and, if possible, with emphatic significance. The line-length is not fixed; most English ballades have been in four-stress lines, iambic or three-part metre. Can our idea survive the preoccupation with form necessary to the composition of a ballade? Probably not. Nevertheless, any writer of verse will gain flexibility by practicing the ballade. And there is always the possibility that he will be able, after several attempts, to strike out a ballade which is also a poem. I make no such claim for this exercise of my own, which I quote to illustrate the form. The line-length, it will be noticed, is five-stress iambic. The diction is deliberately archaic. I believe that no rhyme sound is repeated:

Lady, to whom all men must come at last
Whether with wine-wet lips or starveling wail,
Behold in me a pilgrim, though I cast
No fardel down, nor weep undone and pale
As would a holy man; I come not frail
But strong of sinew, with my bow still bent,
My arrow poised, my body bright as mail,
For I am weary and would lie content.

I do not sue thee ragged and aghast,
But as a prince to purchase thine avail.
Behold, I bring with me a wealth so vast
That seeking it, Phoenician keels might sail
Forever over gloaming waves, and fail.
All thine, if in that nether continent
Grey-cliffed with wanhope, thou canst hear my hail,
For I am weary and would lie content.

Here then I give thee back the child thou wast,
Shut so long in my heart as in a gaol;
Lo, tiptoe on the threshold of the past
She hears again the cloudy nightingale
And sees me glimmer toward her down the dale
And follows me, love with her lover blent,—
Ah, thou rememberest? but do not quail,
For I am weary and would lie content.

Once more, O Lady, thou hast heard the tale,
The gift of days once more received and spent;
Fill thou with wine of sleep this darker grail,
For I am weary and would lie content.

There is no doubt that the ballade has been the inspiration of many stanza forms in the works of poets, even Chaucer, who have studied it. A good example of such influence may be found in Ernest Dowson's *"Non sum qualis eram bonae sub regno Cynaræ."*

Ernest Dowson also wrote some excellent villanelles, a form which seldom displays more than an engaging charm. It is built on two rhyme sounds and the alternate introduction into three line stanzas of two refrain lines which are combined at the end of the poem into a double refrain. Since a good example will serve us better than a chart, I quote Oscar Wilde's "Theocritus," which, although marred by double-weak rhymes, such as the combination of *Persephone* and *Sicily,* yet shows the delightful, if minor, lyrical effects of which the villanelle is capable:

> O Singer of Persephone!
> In the dim meadows desolate
> Dost thou remember Sicily?
>
> Still through the ivy flits the bee
> Where Amaryllis lies in state;
> O Singer of Persephone!
>
> Simætha calls on Hecate
> And hears the wild dogs at the gate;
> Dost thou remember Sicily?
>
> Still by the light and laughing sea
> Poor Polypheme bemoans his fate;
> O Singer of Persephone!
>
> And still in boyish rivalry
> Young Daphnis challenges his mate;
> Dost thou remember Sicily?

Slim Lacon keeps a goat for thee,
For thee the jocund shepherds wait;
O Singer of Persephone!
Dost thou remember Sicily?

Repetition plays a large part in these old forms. They are at their best when every new repetition of a line or a phrase conveys a fresh significance. In the rondeau, a fifteen line form, we have again only two rhyme sounds, and a refrain consisting of the first half of the first line. The rondeau, nearly always found in four-stress iambic lines, has the following scheme: *a a b b a a a b refrain a a b b a refrain*. The most famous rondeau of recent years, correct in form as well as popular, is John McCrae's "In Flanders Fields":

In Flanders fields the poppies blow
Between the crosses, row on row,
That mark our place, and in the sky,
The larks, still bravely singing, fly,
Scarce heard amid the guns below.

We are the dead; short days ago
We lived, felt dawn, saw sunset glow,
Loved and were loved, and now we lie
  In Flanders fields.

Take up our quarrel with the foe!
To you from failing hands we throw
The torch; be yours to hold it high!
If ye break faith with us who die,
We shall not sleep, though poppies grow
  In Flanders fields.

Slightest of all these French forms is the triolet, the small scope of which, as well as the intricate scheme, unfits it for serious employment. Here again we find the double refrain. Of the eight lines, five are repetitions. The god of cleverness may claim the triolet as his own; no other deity, and certainly no muse, will have anything to do with it. First there are two lines (capital letters indicate exact repetitions), then a line rhyming *a,* then *A* repeated, then another line rhyming *a,* then a line rhyming *b,* then lines *A* and *B* repeated in double refrain and, if possible, with a new significance. Although Austin Dobson's triolet does not fulfill the last requirement, it is probably the most famous of our verses in this form:

> I intended an Ode,
> And it turned to a Sonnet.
> It began *à la mode,*
> I intended an Ode;
> But Rose crossed the road
> In her latest new bonnet;
> I intended an Ode;
> And it turned to a Sonnet.

There are several other French forms which might properly be dealt with here, but those we have discussed must stand as typical. With the triolet we have crossed far beyond the line which separates art from artifice. Certainly the ballade and the rondeau may be employed with success. Even the villanelle may encase a lyric of some power, as in E. A. Robinson's fine poem,

"The House on the Hill." But exercises should include at least the possibility of definite achievement. Therefore, although I urge practice in the sonnet and trial of the ballade and the rondeau, I will not counsel the investigation of the more complicated patterns. I have known writers of verse to become hypnotized by these forms as by a jig-saw puzzle, and, in the delight of cleverly designing a sestina or a rondel, to lose all natural sense of poetry. They are like pianists who acquire such unprecedented skill in the playing of scales that they finally become unwilling to proceed to great music.

CHAPTER 7

THE ODE

ODE is one of the most indefinite terms in English verse. Almost any poem of fair length and elevated subject matter may be called an ode. Yet an analysis of the various works in this class reveals three distinct types, which we may name the Stanzaic Ode, the Pindaric Ode, and the Irregular Ode. Since these poems are too long for quotation here, I will refer my readers to the *Oxford Book of English Verse,* in which will be found all the poems I shall cite as examples.

The Stanzaic Ode was originally an attempt in English to reproduce the effect of the Latin odes of Horace. It is a series of stanzas in similar form. Andrew Marvell's "Horatian Ode upon Cromwell's Return from Ireland" is a fair example; so is Collins' "Ode to Evening," one of the finest unrhymed poems in our language. In this ode, so delicate in sound, so rich in imagery, our ears are gratified in spite of the absence of rhyme. No unrhymed lyric except Campion's "Rosecheek'd Laura, come," until Tennyson's "Tears, Idle Tears" can be compared with Collins' lovely ode. The Stanzaic Ode, however, is generally much more complicated in pattern. Spenser's "Prothalamion" and

"Epithalamion" might well have been termed odes. With the four golden odes of Keats,—"On Melancholy," "Autumn," "On a Grecian Urn," and "To a Nightingale,"—the Stanzaic Ode becomes established in full perfection.

The Pindaric Ode is an attempt to reproduce in English the choric ode of the Greek poet Pindar. The basic form is tripartite, consisting of a strophe and an antistrophe (two stanzas identical in form) and an epode (a third stanza differing in form from the first two). This pattern is then repeated any number of times, all the strophes and antistrophes throughout the poem being identical in form, and all the epodes corresponding in like manner. The Pindaric Ode is too complex for general use. An early example is Ben Jonson's "Ode to the Immortal Memory and Friendship of that Noble Pair, Sir Lucius Carey and Sir H. Morrison." The grandest of our Pindaric Odes are Thomas Gray's "The Bard" and "The Progress of Poesy."

The Irregular Ode had its origin in a misunderstanding of the Pindaric form. The seventeenth century poet Cowley failed to recognize the identical correspondence between the various divisions of the Pindaric Ode, and invented a form in which repetition of set patterns plays no part. Dryden followed suit with his "Song for St. Cecilia's Day" and his "Alexander's Feast." The best known of these irregular odes is undoubtedly Wordsworth's "Ode on the Intimations of Immortality from Recollections of Early Childhood," wherein the shifting music skillfully and faithfully follows the shifting mood. So successful is the modulated verse of Wordsworth's poem that we frequently hear this form spoken of as the Romantic Ode.

Modulated verse,—a term I have invented to describe poems wherein lines are of unequal length and rhymes are placed irregularly,—the offshoot of the Irregular Ode, has a distinguished place in English prosody. Milton's *Lycidas* is an early example. It should be noted, however, that a thorough mastery of the set forms is prerequisite to the mastery of this more flexible technique, for they alone can train the ear to detect flaws in the music, and the mind to exercise that proper economy which forbids prolixity. In modulated verse we divide our poem according to the division of thought, we vary our line length according to the amount of content, and we insert our rhymes wherever they most musically and naturally fall. Our modulations from one line length or metre to another must be smooth, and similar rhyme sounds must not be separated by more than four lines, for in longer intervals the sound is lost. Modulated verse may be used very effectively in a short poem, such as Matthew Arnold's "Dover Beach":

> The sea is calm tonight.
> The tide is full, the moon lies fair
> Upon the straits;—on the French coast the light
> Gleams and is gone; the cliffs of England stand,
> Glimmering and vast, out in the tranquil bay.

Come to the window, sweet is the night-air!
Only, from the long line of spray
Where the sea meets the moon-blanch'd land,
Listen! you hear the grating roar
Of pebbles which the waves draw back, and fling,
At their return, up the high strand,
Begin, and cease, and then again begin,
With tremulous cadence slow, and bring
The eternal note of sadness in.

Sophocles long ago
Heard it on the Ægæan, and it brought
Into his mind the turbid ebb and flow
Of human misery; we
Find also in the sound a thought,
Hearing it by this distant northern sea.

The Sea of Faith
Was once, too, at the full, and round earth's shore
Lay like the folds of a bright girdle furl'd.
But now I only hear
Its melancholy, long, withdrawing roar,
Retreating, to the breath
Of the night-wind, down the vast edges drear
And naked shingles of the world.

Ah, love, let us be true
To one another! for the world, which seems
To lie before us like a land of dreams,
So various, so beautiful, so new,
Hath really neither joy, nor love, nor light,
Nor certitude, nor peace, nor help for pain;
And we are here as on a darkling plain
Swept with confused alarms of struggle and flight
Where ignorant armies clash by night.

This poem illustrates well the power of modulated verse in a fairly short passage. In composing this kind of poem it is well to bear in mind that five-stress lines and four-stress lines are usually awkward when juxtaposed (a general principle to which exceptions can be found frequently—in "Dover Beach," for example) and also to bear in mind the old rule: Rhyme everything or nothing.

CHAPTER 8

TEMPERAMENT

EVER since the Romantic Era, a conception of the poet has come into being which may be seen at its least objectionable on the comic stage and at its most objectionable in any large gathering of modern poets. It is a sad fact that poets have earned the reputation for foolishness with which the public has rewarded them. The rolling eye, the flung mass of hair, the absurd elocution, are no mere fancies; I have seen them within a few months on the lecture platform. They are among the symptoms of egotism which manifests itself in many ways.

Naturally, I do not intend to deal with eccentricities of dress and manner. I intend, rather, to discuss certain states of mind which sometimes show themselves in such externalities. Much of the correspondence addressed to one in an editorial position is straightforward and interesting, but the larger part of it, I regret to say, shows rather a strong undercurrent of egotism. There is more often an appeal for advice on how to make oneself known than for advice on how to make the most of one's powers. Publication seems the great end in view, not composition itself. And I must wonder what the result would be if all poets were compelled to publish anonymously. Note well that some of the greatest lyrics in our language, such as "Weep you no more, sad fountain," and the thirteenth century "Hymn to the Virgin" are anonymous, and that not until comparatively recent times have poets considered their work in the light of a vehicle for *self*-expression.

It is very easy to prove the foolishness of self-expression. The self is only important in so far as it can be communicated to other selves. The emotion of an individual is only important in so far as it is the emotion of the race. Suppose a man with poetic talent has a peculiar mania for collecting tomato cans. He will compose love-sonnets to the tomato cans, elegies for the loss of one of his favorites, great comedies and tragedies about them. His work, furthermore, will be worthy of most of the adjectives which today are sought after as high praise: it will be *original,* it will be *striking,* it will be *unique.* And, as poetry, it will be completely valueless, because no one without a passion for tomato cans will be able to share the poet's emotion. This is absurd enough, even as an example, yet many modern poets are employing the underlying method. They are engaged in expressing themselves without any care as to whether or not their ideas are comprehensible even to a few other people. Since the ideal poetry would be the expression of a universal idea or emotion in universal terms, such poets may justly be accused of indulging their egos to the limit.

I am not, however, arguing for the banal, the trite. The poet's job is indeed to set forth an idea or emotion shared by the majority of the race, but he must present it intensely, in concentrated and heightened form. It is just here that his own temperament may play a legitimate part. The true poetic temperament is that faculty which perceives the most ordinary events of life as something wonderful and interesting, the most ordinary objects of life as something beautiful or significant. Without for a moment losing sight of that existence which he shares with his kind, the poet will, at the same time, observe it with a greater excitement than others and from a larger perspective. In like manner, he uses the same words as the rest of his race, but in rarer and more suggestive combinations. To change the figure: in the house of life the poet is the stained glass window which transmits sunlight, like the other windows, yet colors it as it passes through. Any poet should rest content with that; no man is great enough to be both the window and the light. And no man should be so small as to be merely a distorting glass.

The ambition to be "original" (in the false sense) has induced many versifiers to adopt strange diction and bizarre forms. The revolutionist who insists that his thoughts are too vast to be "trammeled" by traditional forms has much to prove. In his case, we again perceive the exaggerated egotism which refuses to comply with universally accepted standards. If every writer is to be a law unto himself, criticism is superfluous, indeed, impossible, and not formal criticism alone, but informal opinion as well. Our objections, our requests for enlightenment are met with the contemptuous "Well, if you can not understand it, I certainly can not explain it." That disposes of us, but only for the time being. For as our numbers increase, we become sufficiently bold to demand an explanation, and if none is forthcoming, we have our own way. Hundreds of forgotten works, the unique products of individuals, may be dug from the ruins of the past by the enterprising seeker.

After all is said and done, the poet's function remains one of the simplest in the world: to lose him*self* in the object he is contemplating, to derive his pleasure from the work he is doing. There is nothing else. Publication is a secondary matter; recognition is nothing, or sometimes, in puffing up the too elastic ego, worse than nothing. Some of the finest poets and the noblest men have received no recognition at all and have not suffered in consequence. One of our most interesting poets, Emily Dickinson, shunned not only publicity but even publication.

The acutest need of modern poetry is an intelligent audience. There are too many poets; and the critics, since the public is too indifferent or ignorant to check critics, are indulging in the maddest riot of personalities, log-rolling, and foolishness in the annals of literature. An intelligent audience would soon put an end to their antics, for it would be better informed than they, and they would fear it. To speak frankly, I hope that my readers will use whatever information they may have derived from these rather random observations, at least as much in the service of criticism as of composition; that they will apply these principles of technique to the work of others as well as to their own.

This brief chapter on Temperament was written in the early 1930's. Now, as 1949 runs out, the situation in poetry is graver than ever. Obsequiously devoted to the pedantry of T. S. Eliot and the incoherences of Ezra Pound, a loose confederacy, with a nucleus of unscholarly reviewers and analysts calling themselves the "New" critics, have seized as much power as has ever fallen into the hands of any band of literary adventurers. Young teachers in the colleges pass on a wholly false set of artistic values to the more precious students who, quite without any foundation in valid learning, assume an arcanic superiority over their less bemused fellows. Early in 1949, a committee of these aesthetes invoked government auspices in order to award a substantial prize to Ezra Pound, whose anti-Semitism and treason to his native country in time of war had been excused on the grounds that he had been declared legally insane. The vulgarity of the aesthetes was only surpassed by their brazen defence of their action. In the controversy that followed, they were brought out into the open and the lines in the artistic and ethical issues at stake were clearly drawn.

CHAPTER 9

REVIEWING VERSE

I⳨ occurs to me that many who read this book may be writing reviews of verse. Even if they are not actually reviewers, they are no doubt called upon frequently to give their opinion on the latest book, and naturally they will wish to do justice to the book and to themselves. So we will turn aside from the discussion of verse and devote a few minutes to criticism.

All critics are agreed that there are three questions to be answered in connection with any work of art: What is the author's purpose? Has he succeeded in it? Is it a creditable purpose? It is apparent that most modern reviewers shirk the asking and answering of these three questions, and so it is that criticism in this country to-day is generally unintelligent and, on the other hand, too emotional. These questions must be answered, directly or indirectly, in every review, because they subject the work under discussion to three sets of standards necessary for a complete appraisal. The first question does justice to the author. It assures a careful reading with a view to establishing the ideas and emotions which the author desired to express. The second question brings to bear the standards of the medium in which the author has expressed himself. These standards are entirely impersonal; they are the result of all experiments that have gone before. The third question returns to the idea or emotion, this time measuring it, not by the author's own standards, but by the standards of humanity. If, after conscientious examination, we cannot answer the first question correctly, then we conclude that the artist is obscure, incomprehensible. If we answer No to the second, then he is not skilful in the style of his art; and if No to the third, then he is an eccentric or a trifler, who has nothing to say worth hearing.

Let us apply these three questions to poetry.

The first question is the most difficult to answer in considering a poem, because so frequently the author's purpose is hidden—even from his conscious self. Thus, we must search further than the apparent purpose in order to find the poetical purpose underlying the whole work. If we remember that whereas prose *states*, poetry *suggests*, we shall be more on the alert. We shall then proceed beyond the mere statements of the poem to find the author's purpose in the suggestions.

Let us take two examples. A careful reading of Holmes's "The Chambered Nautilus" will show us that every figure and phrase in the poem is devoted to the "moral" expressed in the last, and the most emphatic,

stanza. The purpose here was to paint such pictures as
should apply directly to the lesson, "Build thee more
stately mansions, O my soul."

We turn to Keats' "Ode on a Grecian Urn." Again,
at the conclusion of the poem we find a moral:

> "Beauty is truth, truth beauty,"—that is all
> Ye know on earth, and all ye need to know.

Are we to say, then, that the author's purpose here was
also the building up of allegorical pictures? Not if we
have read carefully. If we have given ourselves to the
poem, we have seen a succession of images, pleasing in
themselves; we have felt a certain melancholy, an agree-
able melancholy, such as we always feel in the presence
of the ephemeral beauty of earth; and we have bal-
anced against this mood the thought that art can give
immortality to passing loveliness. Our senses, our emo-
tions, our mind, all are addressed in the polyphony of
the "Ode," and all are stimulated. Furthermore, the
poem is moving, not static. The final development is in
the thought, "Beauty is truth," and so forth, but this is
by no means the purpose of the whole poem, any more
than the final chord is the purpose of a symphony. It
merely provides a dignified conclusion. Taking all this
into consideration, we remark that whereas "The Cham-
bered Nautilus" is a poem with a moral, the "Ode on
a Grecian Urn" is a poem with a mood. That was the
author's purpose: to communicate a mood in which our
senses, emotions, and mind should all be involved.

What is the author's purpose in "Kubla Khan"? In Landor's "Past ruin'd Ilion Helen lives"? In Burns's "A Red, Red Rose"?

Not all poems, in fact very few poems, are as polyphonic as Keats' "Ode." Very often an author will intend to stimulate but one side of our nature. Thus, "Kubla Khan" has to do only with the senses—by the incantation of the verse and the pictures it presents to the inner eye. Landor's epigram is addressed to the mind; Burns's lyric, to the heart. Of course, all poetry, by its form, must involve the senses to some extent; therefore, we always discover some "sensuous appeal." We must distinguish between the sensuous element in the nature of poetry itself and that in the purpose of the author. For example, sensuous appeal plays little part in the satires of Alexander Pope. On the other hand, it is by far the dominant element in the imagistic poems of Amy Lowell.

Until we have established the exact intention of the poet, we can not proceed to the next question: Has the poet succeeded in his intention?

Now we come to all the impersonal standards of the art of poetry. We must consider the phrasing, the metre, the rhythm, the rhyming, the figures of speech, the verbal felicity. What sort of *maker* is this poet? We shall probably have to judge his work, too, by the requirements of different set forms he has employed. Has he written sonnets? We know the rules for the various sonnet forms, and we must discover whether or not he has complied with them. Yet this is not enough. It may be he has broken the rules in several instances. We can not rush to any verdict of Guilty as soon as we discover that fact. We must decide whether or not he has violated the rules intentionally. Someone has described a gentleman as a man who is never *unintentionally* rude. A good writer very often violates the set rules even of so definitely established a form as the sonnet. Now if he has done so deliberately, we must determine whether or not his deviation from the norm justifies his experiment. For example, it has long been considered bad practice to write an iambic pentameter consisting of ten monosyllables. Pope has made fun of such clumsiness thus:

And ten low words oft creep in one dull line.

Very well, there is the rule. Turn to Drayton's sonnet, "Since there's no help, come, let us kiss and part"— one of the finest poems in this form. Each of the first three lines is made up of ten monosyllables. There are many poets who never broke a rule and yet never composed a memorable line; scarcely any great poet—if, indeed, any at all—has been rule-perfect. Let us not swing to a hasty conclusion that breaking rules is a virtue. By no means. But we must bear in mind that there is a double standard in literature: first, the set rule, which constitutes the norm; second, deviation from the set rule, which heightens the main effect of the poem as a whole. Finally, in considering these mat-

ters, we may come to the legitimate conclusion that
although the poem, with all its technical faults, is
noble, it would be better if the rules had not been
broken. But this decision I recommend only to such
experts as think they could suggest improvements!

In connection with this second question, too, we
must consider the sensuous element, already referred
to, which is inherent in the art of poetry. Are the
images merely embellishments, or are they, as they
should be, part of the general structure? Is the verse
musical? Are we moved by the sound of the words
even without trying to understand the meaning?

So many technical matters adhere to the second ques-
tion that I must refer my readers to the entire first part
of this book.

The third question, too, requires a broad answer, and
with this subject we have dealt before. Was the au-
thor's intention creditable? Worth our while? A cred-
itable intention will be to communicate a fine emotion
or idea to as large a number of fellow human beings
as possible. A poet who desires merely to express his
own idiosyncrasies without reference to general human
experience is no poet at all, but an exhibitionist. All art
is more or less excellent as its intention is more or less
communal, so long as it is addressed to the deeper emo-
tions, feelings, and thoughts of the community. A
verse writer may win fame and money by publishing
sentimental ditties which are vastly popular and yet
stimulate only the cheaper minds and hearts. Such a

man is negligible. At the other extreme is the egotist who expects the world to be interested in his eccentricities of emotion or thought.

A lack in the community itself prevents great art from taking hold of the majority of people. Therefore, we must modify our reading of the word communal. The community of poetry is the public which will respond to emotions, sensations, and thoughts expressed in poetic form. As we attempt to define this public, we are forced to become vague because we are at the other end of another puzzling definition, that of poetry itself. What is poetry? Tell me what it is, and I will tell you the sort of person who will respond to it.

Therefore, we must admit that the correct answering of this third question depends on the critical talent of the answerer. A critic with shallow emotions will aver that Mr. Edgar Guest's intention is excellent. A critic who likes nothing but "rattling good stories" in verse will certainly have no quarrel with Mr. Robert Service's poetic purpose. A critic who admires only the things that make him laugh, will insist that the intention of all comic verse is thoroughly artistic. All our prejudices, our tastes, our environment and our heredity are involved when we would answer the third question.

Practically, what can we do about it? I can give only counsel of perfection. First, read widely, so that even though you can not define it, you will know the poetic intention when you see it. No one can define life, but everyone can live wisely through experience. You must experience poetry before you can profitably judge it. Secondly, as soon as you deliver an opinion, examine it to make sure no fluff of prejudice or personal irritation is clinging to it. I suggest doing this after giving the opinion, because it is humanly easier to revise an opinion than to suppress it altogether. If you are writing, all you have to do is to use an eraser; if you are talking, you can eat your words. No diet is so strengthening to moral fibre as one's own words. Lastly, if you feel you are not competent to decide whether or not the author's intention is creditable, answer the first two questions as conscientiously as you can, and frankly confess your inability to answer the third. Tell your reader to decide that for himself. He will, anyway, even though you speak with the tongues of angels.

Few things are more misleading to the student of modern poetry than the average reviews of verse to be found in the book sections of the newspapers. With the exception of the special articles, which are generally assigned to writers who know something about their subject, nearly all the criticism one reads is ignorant, if not perverse. The best poetry seldom reveals its full measure of beauty at the first reading; rather, it continues to unfold with familiarity, and after years still impresses one with new and surprising loveliness. Particularly is this true of lyric poetry. For example, many of the shorter poems of the Elizabethans, of Blake, of Bridges, scarcely touch one, except by their verbal music, at the first reading. After a while, one begins to hear the secondary voices, and only after committing the lines by heart from long familiarity, does one appreciate their significance. Such study is, of course, denied to the ordinary book reviewer. A modern lyric poet is lucky if his book is read through even once before judgment.

Thus, one would be very unwise to follow the condemnations and eulogies of the journalists. At their least harmful, they cover their ignorance in vague phrasing—"Miss Camphire's outpourings breathe forth a spirit of mystical ecstasy, partly idealistic, partly earthly, through which we hear the beat of a human heart and the fluttering wings of a human soul." At their most harmful, they make a dogma of their ignorance—"Mr. Roraback is to be praised for his startling originality. He is individual both in thought and expression. Here is complete freedom from tradition."

In an earlier section of this book, I have already dealt with the fallacy of "startling originality," but the question is so important that I may be excused for presenting a summary.

Originality, in the sense intended by reviewers, is not to be sought after, but eschewed. True originality is almost synonymous with sincerity; it implies, merely, that the writer was indeed the origin of the emotion or idea expressed. It may be a thought which has been expressed hundreds of times before. It will almost surely be just that. Nearly every human being has at

some time experienced love, yet no poet can be con-
demned for writing about love as long as he has actually
experienced it. If he has not done so, and still insists
on writing about it, then he will have to imitate the
writings of those who have experienced it; then, in
truth, he will lack originality. But no subject is hack-
neyed which has its source in the mind or heart of the
one who expresses it.

The false originality, so much praised by the review-
ers, becomes merely the attempt to be different. Of
these two fragments, which seems to you the more
truly original (more sincerely felt)?

1

O western wind, when wilt thou blow
That the small rain down can rain?
Christ, that my love were in my arms
And I in my bed again!

2

You order a chocolate soda
I also
The boy brings them

With bent head
You ply a straw. . . .

You finish your soda
Your head lifts
With a smile. . . .

As for me
To gaze at you

Is chocolate enough
And more than enough

The second is the more startling and individual of the two; yet the first is far fresher, in spite of the archaic *thou* and other devices. Furthermore, the first author was certainly the origin of the emotion he expresses, whereas the second is just as certainly striving for an effect. He is posing in words.

True originality is a combination of three elements: a common speech, a common emotion, and an individual. Note that the individual has a right to but one third of the whole. It is his function to permeate the other two thirds.

The second current fallacy in book reviewing is closely bound up with the first. We find a growing insistence on the part of reviewers that verse be "American." Just what this means I am not quite sure, but we may at least examine the possible meanings.

In the first place, do we find an implication that there is a difference between the English and American languages? Possibly. Yet in spite of much artificial respiration, the American "language" as such remains a dead issue. There is far less difference between American and English speech in general than between the speech of Dorset and London, Kent and Yorkshire. We Americans often phrase things differently from the English; we have retained in currency some words which they have abandoned, and invented a few new ones; our slang differs from English slang. But all these are unessentials. The fact remains that our language is the same as theirs. Of course, we have our own method of vulgarizing or corrupting the language, but the worst dialect of "Noo Yoik," the most bumbling *r* of the Middle West, is no further from good English than the speech of the London Cockney or the super-Cockney of the professional Oxford man. All tongues show local dialects and strata of correctness and vulgarity, but to demand a new linguistic title for each of these would be absurd. If there is an American language apart from English, then there is also a London language, a Dorset language, a San Francisco language, a South Carolina language, and a Chicago language.

Whether we wish to or not we do (and it seems to me our great good fortune) employ the English language. How, then, shall poetry in that language fail to be of the English tradition? A tradition can not be created over night, even in the sanctum of a poetry magazine. We may rebel against the English tradition, we may embellish it with new experiment, for such has always been the way of poets, but we can not do away with it. It is our foundation of a thousand years' building. Not even the abandonment of rhyme and metre denotes a departure from the English tradition. That experiment has been performed many times before this age, and in the beginning it was no experiment but the normal verse. So-called "cadenced verse" is a branch on the main tree which bursts into bloom from time to time. It might be called the century plant of English tradition. It is an exotic, a valuable exotic, of no great importance in itself but refreshing to the perennial stem. There can, in fact, be no American tradition in English verse unless there be a separate American language, and, as we have noted, that theory is false. I sometimes think that our insistence on this nonentity shows an unworthy provincial jealousy. The poet writing in Chicago or Jacksonville does not like his work to be called "English." If that is all, then let us merely settle the argument, as most arguments are settled, by juggling names. Let us call our technique the Pre-American tradition and have done with the question. The Venerable Bede relegated the entire ancient world to B. C. at a time when the years of Our Lord numbered but one third of those before Him. Perhaps we Americans had best start a new calendar beginning in 1492.

Probably, however, our reviewers do not mean dialect and free verse when they praise the "American" qualities of some work. Perhaps they mean the material and setting. A poem about an engine room in Los Angeles will be an American poem because it deals with a modern subject in an American locality; a poem about God speaking from a thundercloud will not be so, because neither God nor the thundercloud has declared his nationality. Had there been book reviewers in the time of King David, I fear things would have gone ill with the author of the Psalms. Doubtless he would have been accused of clinging to the Philistine tradition. Yet somehow, his psalms still seem to satisfy an age and country so far from his as to be unimaginable to him.

The truth is that the less local a work is, the better are its chances of being poetry. Of all limitations, time and space are those first discarded by the intelligent artist. Was Shakspere un-English because he set his plays in Italy, in Scotland, in the Bermudas—almost anywhere but England? Consider the stirring historical events of the Elizabethan Age, and then consider that scarcely one major poet treated of them at all. Think of Edmund Spenser, who deliberately used a language archaic to his own time. Except for Ben Jonson, who adjudged him the meaner poet for that? Is John Drinkwater an American poet because his two best works deal with Abraham Lincoln and Robert E. Lee? This attempt to bind our poetry to our own age and country is one of the most pestilent heresies we have yet endured.

We must be true to our country, not in time and space, but as a countryside. Let not American poets set nightingales to singing in the California woods or plant lotuses in New Hampshire lakes. But, on the other hand, let them not pretend that we have brought into being a new language, a new versification, a new set of human emotions, different from and superior to all that have gone before.

Observation gives us the surface of things; imagination penetrates them. Very often, in the history of the world, an artist finds himself displeased with the surface of things, and, aware that the underlying meaning must be the same in all ages and countries, he chooses a different surface from the one he beholds around him. It was once contended that great tragedy must be written around great figures; that kings and queens were the most appropriate personages for that form of art. Such limitation is unnecessary, but we easily see the purpose of it. The kings and queens are subject to all the human emotions and at the same time present a sufficiently exalted exterior to heighten our interest and sharpen our feelings for their doom. The contrast between their splendid trappings and their unhappy destiny brings into relief all the emotional values of the tragedy. Writers are seldom courtiers, and they must, therefore, rely on their imagination for the portrayal of royalty. The human being beneath the cloth of gold they have observed every moment of their lives.

The "escape," then, is generally into an unusual setting. It may also be into some setting which, through all the mutations of history, remains unchanged.

> Sophocles long ago
> Heard it on the Ægæan,

wrote Matthew Arnold of the sounds of ocean. And Keats, writing of the nightingale's song, says of it:

> No hungry generations tread thee down;
> The voice I hear this passing night was heard
> In ancient days by emperor and clown:

Perhaps the self-same song that found a path
Through the sad heart of Ruth, when, sick for home,
   She stood in tears amid the alien corn. . . .

The seas, the mountains, the forest, the winds, these
things have not changed in all the history of man.
What more natural territory, then, for the poet, whose
instinct is always to contrast the changes of a single life
with the immutable background against which man
moves and has his being? The flight into nature is for
him the most natural of all paths, yet the average re-
viewers of today call on the poet to attempt a feat
wholly uncongenial to his character: the song of sky-
scrapers, jazz bands, dynamos, and politics. If he fails
to conform and from the modern city flies to the time-
less country, he is promptly accused of a surrender, of
a flight from the material that confronts him. The en-
during phenomena are frowned upon as the outworn
machinery of poetry. Can you imagine a hill which is
out of date—a sea out of fashion? Yet so they are, if the
reviewers are to be believed. Of course, we need not
believe them.

We often discover that the writers who are intent
on reflecting the exact conditions around them become
so absorbed in this task that they have neither energy
nor inspiration left for an interpretation of these con-
ditions. Truly, although they are realists in the com-
mon sense of the term, they are escaping from reality.
Of the two elements, surface and meaning, certainly the
latter is the more important. It very frequently happens,

then, that the so-called literature of escape, by leading us far from the confusing actualities around us, brings us face to face with life itself. A parable or a fairy tale will sometimes be far more profoundly accurate than a day-to-day record of events in a mid-western suburb.

CHAPTER 10

SPECIFIC CRITICISM

Now I shall criticize a number of poems which have been sent to me for analysis. The genial authors have sacrificed their works to the public good, and I regret that my thanks to them must be anonymous.

Two of these poems afford an interesting contrast; the first is packed with thought but fumbles the expression of it; the second, in which music is the sole aim, is almost devoid of meaning. If the two authors of these verses could be combined into one, retaining the thoughtfulness of the first and the feeling for melody of the second, we should have a well-rounded poet.

1	The smallest gesture of the past
2	If only long enough ago,
3	Becomes a giant shadow cast
4	Upon our wilderness of snow.
5	The kitchen midden built of waste
6	Becomes the goal of later roads;
7	Its oyster shells, to later taste,
8	More than historic episodes.
9	O life compounded of so much
10	And of so little worth,

11   Behold, the future years shall clutch
12   Thy wreckage from the earth.

On first reading, we notice at once that the author has failed to carry out his pattern. He establishes a four-stress quatrain in the first stanza, holds to it in the second, and in the third suddenly shifts to ballad metre, shortening his tenth and twelfth lines. This change is particularly unfortunate, because when the reader's attention should be wholly focused on the climax of the idea, he is distracted by a break in the form.

The first line of the poem is clear and adequate, but the second is mere prose. The pedestrian quality of the second line becomes even more emphasized by the contrast with the two lines that follow. These employ suggestion or symbolism very markedly and introduce a metaphor which, were its application clearer and were it more in harmony with the preceding tone of the stanza, would be effectve. Yet I am still in doubt about "our wilderness of snow." Does this figure refer to history? to time? to the wintry realism of the present? Here it would be well, I believe, to make a concession to the reader and specify the exact application of the symbol.

The second stanza is specific enough, but again, in the abrupt drop from ornamented language to flat statement, breaks the tone of the poem. "Built of waste" is prosaic and awkward, and not quite accurate. Kitchen middens accumulated; they were not built. In the last two lines of this stanza, the contrast between "oyster shells" and "historic episodes" is effective, yet the phrase "to later taste" is unfortunate in connection with oyster shells; it suggests a sampling of these relics.

In the third stanza, we find an attempt to link together all the general observations in the first two stanzas, and apply them to the life of the present. The idea is good: since even the smallest remains of the past are of significance, perhaps these apparently futile pursuits of life will hold some meaning for later ages. But the expression collapses. The first two lines do not make sense. The author intended to say: O life compounded of so much, and of so little that has any worth. What he has said is: O life compounded . . . of so little worth. The last two lines, which should be the finest in the whole poem, are weak. The rhetorical *behold,* the inappropriate verb *clutch* (to rhyme with *much,* I fear), the rather vague word *wreckage,* and the departure from the established pattern, mar this stanza beyond redemption in its present form.

To sum up: we have here an epigrammatic poem (influenced, I believe, by Emily Dickinson) which is not so terse and neat as an epigrammatic poem must be. The idea is excellent, the general arrangement of it is effective, but in the details of composition the verse is too faulty for successful expression. It needs to be rewritten, every word scrutinized with critical attention.

Now for the second poem:

1   Over fields to the westward horizons are dark
2   And the sunset is dead on the hill.

3 Farewell to the swallow, farewell to the lark,
4   It is dawn for the loud whippoorwill.

5 And the lonely feet treading the edge of the wood
6   Grow slower in pace for a while,
7 As an ecstasy born of the green solitude
8   Stealeth over his face in a smile.

9 The stars to the zenith, the bird to his nest,
10   The snake to his hole in the wall;
11 And lonely feet hasten toward home and toward rest
12   And the whippoorwill reigns over all.

Although these verses, because of great infelicity of
diction, seem very inferior to the others, yet they pos-
sess certain virtues which the others lack. In the first
place, the tone is more evenly sustained. The stanzas
are consistent, and the three-part music, though awk-
ward in spots, is, on the whole, managed with some
skill. Lines 7, 8, and 12 are conspicuously bad; the first
stanza, line 5 and line 9 are fairly successful. But when
we examine the poem more carefully, alas for the first
two lines. The author is so entranced with his music
that he pays too little heed to what he is saying. The
fields to the westward immediately give us a picture of
a flat land, yet we are told in the next verse that "the
sunset is dead on the hill." Now the sunset can be only
in the west; what has happened to our fields stretching
to the horizon? The introduction of the day and night
birds is all very well; it impresses us neither one way nor
the other. However, since the melody is smooth, we are
still tempted to read on. Lonely feet treading the edge

of a wood are effective enough as a sketch of something
to be amplified later. But they are amplified only in the
writer's mind, and suddenly we are confronted with a
smile on *his* face. Who is he? Is his name Lonely Feet?
Furthermore, the vague word *ecstasy* annoys us, and the
insertion of the archaic form *stealeth*. By the end of the
second stanza, we are almost convinced that this author
is wasting our time. He has had two chances; his first
words have attracted our attention in both cases, yet each
time he has wandered off into verbiage. "The stars to
the zenith, the bird to his nest," though in no way re-
markable, bids us read on, and for the third time we are
disappointed. We know so little of Lonely Feet that we
do not care where he goes or why; it is natural that he
should go toward home and toward rest, for he has done
just that in every poem he has ever inhabited. As for
the whippoorwill, he is welcome to reign over *all;* such
a vague kingdom as that is not going to make anyone
envious.

This poem is not worth rewriting because it includes
no idea sufficiently important for re-expression. It must
stand or fall by its melody alone, and since that is im-
perfect, it must be considered as a practice piece in prep-
aration for something better. It would be profitable for
the author of this second poem to try his hand at re-
writing the first; the contact with a specific idea would
do him a world of good. And I should judge that he
is not quite ready yet to employ three-part metre, for,
though his verses are smooth and fairly sonorous, they

do not exhibit much variation. And as I have said before in connection with the three-part metres, skilful variation is their one requirement.

Now we analyze a narrative poem entitled "Paradise," which deals with the life of a brother and sister. The climax of the story is his death in the late war. Up to that point, the diction was simple and crisp, the emotion was held in restraint, and the treatment in general was unaffected and straightforward. But at the climax—and here is a familiar weakness in modern verse—the author distrusted his own powers; he ceased to record the situation at first hand, and fell back on a second-hand phraseology which, since it had been used again and again to stimulate emotion, he thought would be serviceable in communicating his own. Of course, it vitiates the whole effect of the work. Let us concede that his emotion was sincere, as it doubtless was. Yet let us remark at the same time how insincere, how trite, are the phrases by which he attempts to communicate it. The boy is described as setting off for "over there," and at his departure, "it braced us all to keep our *heart throbs* hid." The soldier speaks of the war thus:

> "Bully scrap! you bet I couldn't bear
> To keep hands off. I'll be back just as soon
> As this job's done" . . .

If any young man spoke of the war thus, it was merely because, like this author, he had read half a dozen novels in which the heroes were made to employ such phrases,

and so he considered them the proper ones for the oc-
casion. After the brother has been killed in France, we
are told that:

"The sky is black, all but a *gold star.*"

Again, the emotional effect of the gold star is second
rate; it cheapens the climax because it brings to mind
the dreary waste of sentimental songs, posters, and war
stories which flourished during the overwrought period
of a great conflict but withered at once in the clear, cold
light of the aftermath. I am in no way implying that
time can diminish the sombre power of the tragedy;
I am pointing out that the war-time symbols of that
tragedy must be discarded for others less shopworn. In
repeating the superficial diction of the war, our author
has destroyed the war's underlying significance, and,
incidentally, capped a good poem with a weak climax.

As it happens, the employment of second-hand
phrases is the prevalent fault in the poems of most young
writers. It seems that in regarding a landscape or under-
going an experience too many versifiers at once concern
themselves, not with what is happening to them, but
with what other poets have said in the same circum-
stances. Note in these first three stanzas of a poem en-
titled "An Alberta Sunrise" how the author begins
simply enough with a fair description of what lies be-
fore him, and then becomes gradually more "literary,"
until his verses are little more than a catalogue of out-
moded poeticisms:

(neuter)	A crimson flush I can descry
(neuter)	Suffusing now the eastern sky,
(neuter)	It spreads, and soon the shades of night
(neuter)	Recede before advancing light.
(fair)	The waning moon, her lustre gone,
(fair)	Yields crown and sceptre at the dawn;
(weak)	The morning star with weak'ning ray
(good)	Turns fainter still, then fades away.
(weak)	Enthralled I gaze on gorgeous view
(weak)	As roseate dawn takes richer hue,
(bad)	In panoply of lambent flame
(bad)	The sun comes forth his throne to claim.
(bad)	Then far and wide o'er 'wakened world
(neuter)	His fiery banners are unfurled;
(bad)	The clouds ablaze seem now to me
(bad)	Like flaming isles in saffron sea.
(bad)	Empyrean heaven's glories bright
(neuter)	Are now revealed to mortal sight
(bad)	And ne'er since Time its course began
(neuter)	Did grander sight greet eye of man!
(weak)	O wondrous pageant of the sky,
(bad)	Symbol of future life on high!
(weak)	Conceived in glory, radiant morn,
(weak)	In fitting splendour thou art born! . . .

Here is a poem smoothly metrical, exalted in feeling, highly coloured. Why, then, are so many of the lines weak or bad? Because the diction is second-hand, third-hand, fourth-hand. Note the artificial contractions: *weak'ning, o'er, 'wakened* (which need not be a contraction anyway), *ne'er.* Note the strained word order: *glories bright, since Time its course began.* And, worst fault of all, the poeticisms: *roseate dawn, panoply, lambent, saffron, empyrean, wondrous, on high,* and many others.

The same author submits a poem entitled "The Dying Year," in which the unhappy results of too "literary" composition are even more manifest, for here with the stock vocabulary he has unconsciously introduced are stock ideas of which that vocabulary is the outward and visible sign. And there lies the greatest danger of second-hand diction; it is sure to bring with it second-hand ideas. Since this author has a well developed metrical sense and a keen perception, his job, it seems to me, is to speak out loud and bold, in his own language, of his own impressions.

Echoes, however, need not always be unfortunate. Sometimes a paraphrase from some older work, deliberately introduced to heighten an effect, may be of great poetic value. In quoting the epigram entitled "Peace," I would call the reader's attention to the deft use, in the second line of the second stanza, of one of the epitaphs from the Greek Anthology:

> Here where the tall grass waves
>   The fallen soldiers lie
> In countless rows of graves
>   Under a sunny sky.
>
> Here where the poppies dance
>   They obeyed the last command;
> And these, they died for France,
>   Those, for the Fatherland.

> They struggle now no more
>   In any hour or weather:
> The best their countries bore
>   Lie down in peace together.

Slightly suggestive of the lyrics of A. E. Housman, this epigram, nevertheless, stands firmly on its own feet. Note that the diction is simple throughout; the author has no verbal tricks, no blurred abstractions. The clearness contributes to its power on second reading. A first reading informs us perfectly of everything the author wishes to say, yet we read it again with renewed pleasure. Simplicity, as always, is the magic. Only once, it seems to me, does this simplicity break down into banality. The author might have chosen another flower than poppies. They have become almost as trite a symbol of emotion as the gold star mentioned in connection with the first poem.

Let us examine a lyric, the stanza form of which is well-turned and musical, influenced, perhaps, by the Elizabethans.

ON THE LAST DAY OF FEBRUARY

1	I found a flower today
2	Hidden away
3	Among the dry, dead leaves of winter.
4	Yellow it was and exquisite
5	The beauty of it
6	Was single; for March had not yet lent her
7	Wealth of golden daffodils,

8   Nor breathed the warmth of spring that fills
9   With violets the wooded hills.

10   Alone in loveliness;
11   Yet I confess
12   No full-blown field seemed lovelier
13   Than that small flower blooming there
14   As it would dare
15   The wind's cold lances that leveled were.
16   Tomorrow perchance the frost will drop
17   Its freezing death into that cup
18   Of beauty, held so bravely up.

Somewhere I have remarked that only perfect music can compensate for a lack of idea; that, on the other hand, we grant to certain poets (Donne, for example) a deal of metrical license because their ideas are strong enough to compensate for a deliberate shaking up of the metre. Now in the poem quoted above, we have a right to expect very fine music indeed, because the content is slight and because the second stanza, instead of developing the thought, merely repeats it. But the music has faults. Line 5 is unmetrical because it fails to bring to the insignificant word *it* sufficient stress; as it stands, the line reads as if it had a feminine ending. A monosyllable should be substituted for *beauty*. Furthermore, there is a violent run-over or enjambment into line 6, which, in turn, runs over into line 7. Trisyllabic feet, such as the one in line 5, are often desirable, as are run-overs from line to line. But lines 5, 6, and 7 show too many irregularities, particularly since they are unmetrical within themselves. The phrase *"lent her"* is a gallant attempt to couple a rhyme with *winter*, but it is too rough and conspicuous to be successful. The beginning of the second stanza illustrates very well the principle that in verse one should preserve the logic of prose. The subject of the first sentence is *I*, and *I*, apparently, is *alone in loveliness*. *Dare*, line 14, in the sense of challenge or defy, seems a concession to the rhyme. Line 15 is awkwardly inverted, and the trisyllabic foot in line 16 is unpleasantly lilting. The two last lines are effective.

To sum up: this lyric should be rewritten in more regular measure and with stronger diction. The feeling is good, and the underlying music; the stanza form itself, ingenious.

There is a lyric in this collection which seems to me much influenced by Emily Dickinson's work, and which, if it has some of the felicity of her greater poems, is weakened at the same time by the obscurity which mars some of her work. Very likely the author of this poem will retort that he has never read Emily Dickinson, and certainly the influence is not so strong as to mar the individuality of the poem.

WORDS

I The longest day must end,
    And even nights of pain;
II Strong-fibred leaves will bend
    Beneath a casual rain.
III To you words are but words,
    To me, prophetic sign,

As swiftly gathering birds
　　May waver into line
　Because of age-old fear.
IV　　One word you flung to me
　Foretold a time too near;
V　　Faith can not live and see
　What bruised and torn lies here
　　To bury or to save. . . .
VI　Which shall it be, my dear,
VII　　And is this all we gave?

Instead of numbering the lines, I have numbered the sections in which the thought is developed. In the first place, we all agree that the versification is skillful, and the diction, for the most part, distinguished. The main difficulty with the poem is that it has more puzzle-element than it is entitled to. Section II is beautifully stated, but just what is its application to I? Section III, again, is clear within itself and illustrated by a good figure of speech, but what is its connection with I, II, or even IV? It is often well to omit the transition between two kindred thoughts; sometimes that method brings great emphasis to bear. But these thoughts seem not kindred, and we soon begin to suspect that this is not one poem but several included in one. However, our ingenuity is challenged and we are pleased with the apt phrasing, so we give the author our best attention through two, three, four readings. And we are still left with several legitimate questions. What is the time foretold in IV? Just where is the *here* referred to in V? We decide that the *which* in VI refers to a choice between burying and saving, but we still do not see the connection with VII. And lastly, in VII, what does *this* refer to? This poem, though interesting and well illustrated, is not clear.

Here is a sonnet by the same author:

PEACE

1 And what of this frail peace men postulate?
2 White moons that fading skies may bring to birth
3 Distill a whiter peace than any earth
4 I cling to now. But since you come so late
5 My way is wide of moons remorseless fate
6 Has hidden for the few. There is no dearth
7 Of love nor am I comfortless, though mirth
8 Delays, whose touch is all-compassionate.
9 Yet laughter with abandoned air shall make
10 Us free of passion's darker ecstasy;
11 There is no easy way of peace. Forsake
12 This dream that stupifies, put out to sea,
13 With fear enchained ride through the leaping wave
14 And from some sky peace may descend to save.

Here again, we find a certain clogging of the thought. The thought-structure of the sonnet, which is the essence of the form, has been ignored. Consequently, we find no reason for the use of the sonnet. Yet the poem is interesting. One suspects its author of being bombarded with ideas during the composition of the poem and of not resisting sufficiently the impulse to include them all. Composition, as may be seen by considering the meaning of the word, precludes the entertainment of unforeseen material. It seems evident to me that this author does not separate, as he should, the three stages in the writing of a poem: observation, recollection, composition. If a new idea, or an important development of the old idea, arrives during composition, it may be jotted down as the nucleus of a second poem, or, if it be sufficiently powerful, it may be substituted for the original poem. It cannot be combined with the original poem after composition has begun—particularly in a sonnet, where the balance of thought is so nice.

In technical detail, I do not find "Peace" so satisfying as "Words." *Postulate* in line 1 is a flat word, and suggests Euclid rather than Petrarch. The symbol of the moon for peace is convincing, but the phrase *"any earth"* suggests that various earths are clung to from time to time. Of course, it becomes obvious that *earth* is used as a symbol for various states of mind, but the second symbol follows the first too quickly. This poet's characteristic is a superabundance of the qualities which most modern writers lack: idea and symbol. Postu*late* in line 1 is an identical rhyme with *late* in line 4. We have already agreed that *postulate* must be changed. In line 5, the omission of the pronoun causes confusion. The line should read (disregarding metre) *"My way is wide of the moons which remorseless fate."* As it stands, we think for a moment that *moons* should be a possessive, and that the apostrophe has been omitted by mistake. The *dearth* and *mirth* of lines 6 and 7 seem used merely for the rhyme's sake and make us suspect padding. In the sestet, again, there is none of that economy which is necessary for the memorable sonnet, and the last line, which should be the strongest, is one of the weakest in the poem. There is much that is interesting and individual in this author's work, but he should be single-minded during the composition of a single poem.

Here is another sonnet which embodies many interesting faults. Interesting faults, by the way, are rare; they are generally found in the work of someone who has the genuine poetic instinct but has not yet conquered the medium of his art. The uninteresting faults, which are in a large majority, are these: total ignorance of poetic form (for example, one author enclosed some jagged, irregular verses which he had entitled a sonnet); sentimentality (hackneyed treatment of hackneyed themes); moralizing (the sort of "keep smiling" verses of which Edgar Guest's effusions are typical); heart throbs (perfervid exposition of one's personal emotions); and cheap humor. The interesting faults, on the other hand, are the slight lapses which mar otherwise careful work.

The sonnet under consideration is entitled "On the Ideal," and at once our attention weakens. To go back to first principles: Abstractions are to be shunned. Whatever the Ideal is, it must be embodied in concrete form, something that can be imagined. It may be embodied as a person, a mountain, a wind, a season, a forest; in any case, it must be definite, else we can not grasp its significance. The reader of this sonnet will subsequently discover that the Ideal is the creative force mov-

ing through nature, and his interest will depend on the
skill of the author in presenting objects which reveal
this force:

1 Thou art my love, I seek thee here or where
2 Beauty's most lovely image may be seen,
3 Where in the breeze the glistening birches are
4 Dancing like nymphs before the hemlock's green.
5 Among the phantom beeches by the brook
6 Awaiting Spring's inspired rhapsody,
7 Yearning within her tender heart I look
8 And hark as for a promised melody.
9 A will o' the wisp art thou, th'inviolate,
10 Holding my vagrant soul a prisoner,
11 Thou art the risen lark at Heaven's gate
12 Singing to thine entrancéd listener.
13 How shall I praise the power that from a clod
14 Creates the man, from man creates the god?

The most serious fault is certainly the thin, abstract
diction. The poem also suffers from weak rhymes, out-
moded elisions and, in line 11, a too clear echo from
Shakspere's Sonnet XXIX. In line 1, the contrast be-
tween *here* and *where* is vague. Line 2 is meaningless
verbiage. Just what is *Beauty's most lovely image?* Is
it a face? a solitary beach? a forest? *We must know.*
Poetry is not a matter of fact, to be sure, but it must pro-
vide material for the sensuous imagination. Lines 3 and
4 are the first indication of power. The picture, though
not startling, does much to redeem the first quatrain.
Again, line 5 suggests the thin, wintry leaves of the
beeches very well, but the image immediately fades in

the vague and hackneyed phrasing of line 6. In line 7, *her* has no antecedent, and the meaningless line is further confused. In line 8, the word melo*dy* forms a double-weak and identical rhyme with rhapso*dy* in line 6. Rhyming can be no worse, unless it is entirely false. In line 9, *th'inviolate* is an unnecessary and cumbersome elision; furthermore, *inviolate* is meaningless. Inviolate to what? Line 10 is harmless; line 11, as has been pointed out, is almost a quotation from Shakspere's sonnet. Line 12 is musical, but again we find a double-weak identical rhyme, liste*ner*. The terminal couplet of the sonnet shows more ability of epigram than we should have expected from the rest of the poem.

Very well, the sonnet is destroyed. What is left? Why consider it at all since it shows so many faults? Because these faults are all obviously part of the apprenticeship of one who really possesses the poetic instinct. Even the too-close adaptation from Shakspere shows a study of models without which no technique can be developed. The construction of the idea is excellent, and the metrical movement of the poem shows a musical ear developed by practice and susceptible of further development. It is apparent that all the weaknesses of the sonnet are on the surface; they are remediable.

The following short lyric shows similar faults and possibilities:

RAIN

1   Rain against my window pane,
2   (Rain against my heart)

3   Blurring outlines in the street.
4   (Blurring pain in part)
5   Silver grey and drooping leaf,
6   Beauty softly clad.
7   (Does this hush within me mean
8   I can yet be glad?)

The first two lines recall too clearly Verlaine's *"Il
pleut sur la ville comme il pleut dans mon coeur."* Line
4, with *part* dragged in so obviously for the sake of
rhyme, is meaningless. Lines 5 and 6 are effective be-
cause the author has given us the image before speaking
of the abstraction (*Beauty*). The last two lines are
prosy. Yet as a whole, the poem has possibilities.

Here is another sonnet:

MY HOUSE

1   A house upon a village hill is mine,
2   (A more than dream-like thing puffed out with air.)
3   It stretches to the four winds staunch and square,
4   And to the south wall clings a jessamine.
5   Ghosts on the north have claimed a trumpet-vine
6   To warn me in what rooms they mean to stare,
7   I do not mind; in fact, I think I'd dare
8   Invite them in on rainy nights to dine.

9   My house holds wistful songs of many spheres,
10 No singer doubts the tale his neighbor tells,
11 No guest there dreads the devil or his spells,
12 Nor frowns upon a startling truth he hears.
13 And so my house means hospitality,
14 God visits there; He likes society.

A pleasantly fantastic, conceited poem, written appropriately in conversational idiom. Technically, it needs much strengthening. In the first place, the figures presented by lines 2 and 3 refer to the same object but contradict each other. The image, therefore, is erased. Line 2 suggests a bubble; so does the verb *stretches.* Why, then, *square?* Our minds had already conceived the image of a sphere. This comment may seem carping, but it applies to a really serious fault: the mixing of images, an enlargement of the old fault of mixed metaphor. Jessa*mine* and *mine* form an identical rhyme. The second quatrain is pleasant and well-turned. In line 9, "Wistful songs of many spheres" might well be strengthened, but, in general, the third quatrain continues the conceit effectively. The terminal couplet, which should be the strongest part of the poem, is the weakest. In the first place, the double-weak, identical rhyme of hospita*lity* with socie*ty* is impossible. In the second place, I complain vigorously against the practice common among budding poets of dragging in God to swell their work when their inspiration is at its lowest ebb. This couplet should be removed, and another, more climactic and more in tone with the rest of the poem, should be substituted.

There has arisen during this century a particularly weak convention in verse. For lack of a better term, we may call it the "gypsy mood." The picture of gypsy life—the camp fire, the shifting seasons and landscapes, the desire ever to set forth into another country—is no doubt poetic enough; certainly it has inspired some excellent writing, both in verse and prose. But of late it has become sadly debased. I suppose the verses of Kipling are largely responsible for this noxious influence. Kipling, an expert short story writer, is by no means a great poet. His lilting rhymes are well enough for those readers who can advance to nothing better, but as a model for beginning poets, he is ruinous. His metrical effects are raw, his ideas are stale, and his sentimentality is unpardonable.

To return to the gypsy mood. This convention has been so overworked that it inevitably forces upon those who employ it all the outworn phrases and monotonous rhythms which cling to it. As an example, I shall quote "Gypsy Longing." Even the title is stale.

> There's a song in the gypsy heart of me
>   Seeking the winding way . . .
> Longing for wind-blown heath and lea
>   And the new-born hush of day.
>
> I'm loving the fragrant blue smoke o' the fire
>   As it curls toward the sheltering sky . . .
> The farther away is a village spire
>   The happier song sing I.
>
> Oh, it's calling, the lure of the open road,
>   The star-lit sky at night,
> To stride along as my fathers strode
>   And to find my soul in flight . . .
>
> To die with the voice of a thrush in my ears,
>   Or the golden lark in song,

With the blessing of Pan throughout many years
And the soul of me growing strong!

There's a song in the gypsy heart of me,
    Wanting the gypsy way—
Breathing on wind-blown heath and lea
    At the ending of the day.

In this poem, we note a curious phenomenon com-
mon to most of these gypsy songs. Although the mood
is supposed to be inspired by that wandering folk of
Bohemian origin, the phrasing is Irish in idiom! *Oh, it's
calling, the lure of the open road* is so Celtic in texture
that we expect the next line to be *To me and my dark
colleen.* Other annoying tricks of this type of writing
are illustrated by the phrases: *heart of me, soul of me,*
instead of *my heart* and *my soul.* As far as I have been
able to discover, this unidiomatic arrangement of the
possessive was invented for the convenience of poets
who find it easier to rhyme with the long *e* sound than
with *heart* or *soul.* We also notice the unpleasant elision
in *blue smoke o' the fire,* which has become inevitable
in such verse. We can hear the phrase sung by a too lush
tenor. Finally, the introduction of Hellenic Pan into
this Bohemian-Celtic style destroys the last possibility of
illusion.

The pity of it is that the author of this poem has facil-
ity, a good ear for lyric effects, and, doubtless, a true feel-
ing for what he is writing about. The epigrammatic

The farther away is a village spire
The happier song sing I,

shows possibilities which are not realized in the present sample of his work. The fact is that he has fallen under a very enervating influence.

I should not deal with this subject so fully and so firmly were I not deluged with poems showing how widespread is this gypsy mood. I need only quote a few titles: "Pipes o' Pan" (the verses were good, but the *o'* threw me off at once); "Gypsy Yearning"; "Gypsy Love"; "Just a Bit o' the West"; "Trail o' Dreams." How is one to pronounce that *o'* anyway? The nearest I can come to it is a grunt.

Another general fault which I have noticed is a tendency to echo too closely the cadence of some well-known poem. No doubt this imitation is unconscious, but its effect is always unfortunate. If the verses recall some really great piece of work, the reader immediately makes comparisons unfavorable to the echo; whereas, if they recall some inferior but popular poem, he concludes that the echo's taste is not so good as it should be. As an example of the first type, I shall quote a stanza which must recall to every reader Gray's "Elegy":

> The vesper bell rings softly from the hill,
>   The weary birds fly homeward from the sky,
> The mist of evening rises gray and chill
>   And all the waking world has passed me by.

Vastly inferior as this is to the great Elegy, its rhythmic measure is so similar that it immediately brings to mind the first stanza of the older poem. The diction and even the mood are different, but the march of the verses, the construction of the sentences, are identical.

Here is another example:

> By Lethe's stream the poppies grow—
> And there my soul will ever be.
> Men care not that thou didst strive
> To raise a great name when alive.
> Thy name is lost in that great sea
> Where millions upon millions go!

We will pass over the awkwardness of the fourth line, the strength of the last two, and the qualities of the stanza in general, to consider the echo in the first line. The word *poppies* has become so intimately related to a certain type of war poetry that we must be very sure it conveys no imitative note. The author of this stanza, far from taking any such precaution, has allowed his first verse to fall into the exact measure of

> In Flanders fields the poppies grow.

This imitation is not plagiarism by any means. Our memory stores up many rhythmic impressions, and it is quite natural that these should be communicated to the mind during composition, along with more original material. I believe, however, that whenever we incorporate an echo into a poem, we are vaguely aware that something is wrong. Perhaps we cannot ourselves find out just where the echo occurs. The solution of this problem is to read any suspected passage to a group of friends and ask them frankly if they find any imitative lines.

It will be noted that both the general faults which I have just mentioned are the result of a too "literary" method of composition. The gypsy mood and the unconscious echo have their source in other people's work. It is not inappropriate, therefore, to repeat at this time the warning that every writer must be in direct contact with his subject. He must not perceive nature, his emotions, or any material in the indirect light shed by some-one else's work.

Self-consciousness is one of the strongest foes of poetry. In an earlier discussion I spoke of the dangers of overestimating one's own experiences, of failing to make them of general interest. In that connection, I mentioned the tendency in modern letters to express an eccentricity as if it were a universal human truth. The personality of the writer should not intrude; its sole function is to intensify some emotion or idea which already is familiar to at least a group of human beings. And therefore an eccentricity, unrelated to normal life, has no proper place in literature. The *self*-consciousness which insists on the importance of the individual in opposition to all the convictions of our kind and the laws of our art is so conspicuous that we recognize it at once and discount it.

But there are other sorts of self-consciousness which have their source not in egotism but in bashfulness. Like a child, shy in the presence of his elders, the novice in poetry is over-careful with his manners. If he meets an unexpected problem he harks back to "good form" rather than to his own experience; he fills in the gaps of his knowledge with mannerisms taken from books; in short, he is merely imitative. From this weakness evolve many of the faults to be observed in the verse of beginners: forced rhymes, hackneyed phrases, echoes from older poets, artificial emotions, stilted metaphors.

THE CLOSE OF A WINTER'S DAY

1 So swiftly sank the winter's sun
2   Beyond the woods, its flushed colour
3 But tinged the sky ere it was done,
4   Leaving a glorified glamour
5   Over the valley, and then twilight
6   That ushers in the stars of night.

7 No sign of life in that valley
8   With its old-fashioned rural homes
9 Did I observe—in road or alley,
10   These folk might dwell in homes of gnomes,
11   I thought, and the cold still grew and lay
12   Crisply at the closing of the day.

13 But ah! the chopping of a log
14   At the far-away edge of the vale,
15 And yip-yap of a persistent dog
16   Broke through the silence that did prevail.
17   Then through the leafless trees of oak
18   Flickered a light and swirled a smoke.

Now, it must be obvious to anyone who has read the preceding pages that there are many technical errors in these verses: forced rhymes, broken metres, and awkwardness in phrasing. Yet certainly the writer knew

what he was talking about; he was moved by his subject
and wished to convey that emotion. Disregarding all
technical difficulties (let the reader annotate those for
himself), just where has the author conveyed his feeling
directly and where has he been too timid to follow his
own muse?

The first three lines are non-committal. With the
word *glorified,* we suspect that the dictionary is the au-
thor, and we are not much reassured by lines 5 and 6.
Line 7 does not interest us, and the *old-fashioned rural
homes* of line 8 suggest the phrasing of a daily news-
paper. Yet the statement *did I observe,* even with its un-
comfortable expletive, commands our attention. Then
the *alley* and the *gnomes,* patently introduced to bolster
up the sagging rhyme, render us almost hostile to the
poet. We read on merely to jeer, but discover in lines 11
and 12 indubitable evidence of sincerity. And except for
the *But ah!* at the beginning, the last stanza is wholly
convincing. The sound of distant chopping, the barking
of the dog,—these details will recall to anyone's mind
the atmosphere of the winter night; they are so well
chosen that they stand as symbols for the entire scene.
And finally, in spite of the awkward *trees of oak,* the
last couplet has some poetry. We are not sure just why,
for we can not thoroughly analyze this quality. We are
certain, however, that the magic would have failed had
the image been blurred ever so slightly by "literary" or
self-conscious handling.

Regarding these three stanzas as a whole, we perceive

that all the poetry is in the last. There are three techni-
cal faults in this passage: the *But ah!;* the *did prevail,*
identically rhyming with *vale;* and the *trees of oak,*
which is not idiomatic English. But we are not dealing
with external qualities at present. We are, rather, deal-
ing with the state of mind favorable to poetry. Let us
work backward from the poem to the author.

It is clear that he was moved by his subject and that he
was near it when he composed the verses. It is equally
clear that after his first line he became self-conscious. As
the difficulties of composition increased, he devoted him-
self to their solution and took his eyes off his subject.
Just so, a self-conscious person in society will conduct a
rapid conversation, and completely forget what he is
talking about, so intent is he on preserving all the
niceties of decorum. Now the poet under discussion was
worried, perhaps without knowing it, by the treason to
his material which he was committing. We find evi-
dences of that in the phrases *did I observe* and *I thought.*
Consciously or unconsciously, he wrote these not for the
sake of the reader but to recall his own attention to his
subject. By the time he reached his last stanza, his tech-
nique had been limbered up by the exercises of compos-
ing the other two; the friction had produced sufficient
heat to stimulate his best efforts. And, if I am reading
his experience correctly, the last stanza "wrote itself."
In other words, the phrasing ceased to trouble him and
he was enabled to concentrate all his attention on what

he had actually seen and heard. What should he have done then?

He should have gone back to the beginning and ploughed up those first two stanzas from end to end with all the force which he had mustered. The momentum of the last stanza would have carried him clear through the poem again.

But poets, after they have just finished a work, are lazy critics. The triumph of the last stanza shed its glow back over the other two, and he saw them in its light. It would have been better to eliminate the first two entirely, leaving the last one to stand alone. For not until the last one did he feel sufficiently at home with the subject he was entertaining to speak in his natural voice, without self-consciousness. And until we are sure that every trace of self-consciousness, of awkwardness, is destroyed, we have no right to inscribe *finis* or *stet*.

Ever since the beginning of poetry, poets have tried to define the phenomena of life in their own terms. The instinct is close to the tendency toward metaphorical language. Metaphor lies halfway between comparison and definition. Someone writes, "My thoughts are like butterflies," a simile, a comparison. Another, "My thoughts are butterflies," a metaphor to convey the quality of one's thoughts. And a third will define his thoughts. Poets have always delighted in all

three forms of speech. Sometimes they cast their defini-
tion in the form of a riddle, embellishing the object they
were describing with all sorts of picturesque and mis-
leading fancies; sometimes they use definition to ex-
press their own opinion of the subject under discussion.
But very seldom can a poem which is definition, and
definition alone, rise to any great height.

The reason is simple. Although poetry may teach,
it must not be written merely to teach. And definition,
since it is always bent to the poet's own ideas, is just
another form of teaching. The most popular verses in
this mode are Kipling's "If," beloved of motto-card
manufacturers, a jingling collection of platitudes, which
too often represent the average man's investigations into
ethics. The best definitions which are also poems are
generally short, epigrammatic, and memorable, "What
oft was thought but ne'er so well expressed." Thomas
Hardy's "Young Man's Epigram on Existence" is one
of these, and many of Emily Dickinson's unforgettable
epigrams belong in the same class.

Among the definitions I have recently received is
this:

WHAT IS LIFE?

What is life? Azure skies and birds,
Butterflies and sunshine, lightsome words
Sung to lilting music, bowers
Of fruits and flowers.

What is life? Clouds and mist by day,
Mist and clouds at night that shroud the way,

Phantom figures that struggling go
To and fro.

A tapestry of gold and sable thread,
A rainbow gleaming when a storm has sped,
Delight, perplexity, and strife—
All this is life.

The verses are well-turned, but we feel that the sub-
ject is covered with that factual thoroughness proper
to prose. Furthermore, the last two lines of the second
stanza are certainly "fillers," and in this form of writ-
ing, above all others, fillers are intolerable. In writing
a definition, we should remember that decoration is
wholly out of place. Terseness, compactness, is the great
aim. This poem should be cut down to four, or at most,
six lines:

What is life? Azure skies and birds,
Butterflies and sunshine, lightsome words,
Phantom forms of cloud and mist by day,
Mist and cloud at night that shroud the way,
Delight, perplexity, and strife—
All this is life.

Of course, the diction should be strengthened, as well
as the construction. It seems rather late still to be
warring against *azure* and *lightsome;* to point out
the interior rhyme of *cloud* and *shroud,* and the hack-
neyed rhyme of *strife* with *life.* Now that the poem
has been shortened, the author should study every
word of the epigram with a view to improvement. The
poem as it originally stood is well above the average

composition of a novice, but being a definition, it demands the utmost polish for its full effect.

Here is another:

> Friendship is a single tone
>   Struck at random by two hearts,
> Neither one could sing alone
>   For the chord required two parts.
>
> Friendship is a single speech
>   Only two can understand.
> All to say and all to teach
>   In the pressure of a hand.
>
> Friendship I have never known
>   And my heart lies on a shelf,
> Singing to itself alone
>   Talking sadly to itself.

In this curiously uneven poem we have evidences of skill, separated by lines and phrases which are *sadly* (to use the author's rather weak word) bungled. The figure in the first stanza is good, but it is not consistent. If the tone is single, how can there be a chord? And note, in the last line of that stanza, the flatness of the word *required*. The second stanza could hardly be improved. It fulfills all the demands of this sort of writing, and, in my opinion, should stand alone. In the last stanza, again we find a clumsiness strongly contrasting with the skill of what has gone before. *My heart lies on its shelf!* What a phrase! Its overtone brings to mind the old slang expression: I've been laid on the shelf. The actual picture is scarcely less unpleasant than the charge made against Mrs. Shelley (she denied it) that she had used her dead husband's mummified heart as a book-mark. And, finally, we know that the shelf was only included to furnish a rhyme for *itself* in the last line.

Why can not a writer of such apparent skill develop his critical powers sufficiently to distinguish and separate the excellent second stanza from the faulty two?

And here is one more definition:

> Love is a sea,
>   A moving tide—
> Eternity
>   In quest of bride;
> A mighty storm
>   Where ships go down,
> An evening calm,
>   A cross, a crown.

Here we meet again the bugbear of all composition, abstraction. The sea—good, a concrete symbol of the abstraction, Love. But, continuing, we find that Love is Eternity, and the two smoky abstractions meet, dilute each other, and vanish in a thin vapor. We return, then, to the sea, and discover that Love is sometimes stormy and sometimes calm. But in the last line where, if anywhere, the epigram should find its logical climax, the sea is suddenly abandoned altogether, and the cross and crown are introduced at the last minute and with unseemly haste. The definition lacks proper construction; we feel that the author is playing with ideas, rather than organizing them into one unified, logical sequence.

Finally, we may add that the best definitions in verse are those which are merely implied. It is generally weak to begin "What is life?" or "Friendship is." The obviousness of the method puts us into a frame of mind for prose, not for poetry. Consider the implied definition in Francis Quarles's "Epigram":

> My soul, sit thou a patient looker-on,
> Judge not the play before the play is done.
> Her plot hath many changes; every day
> Speaks a new scene; the last act crowns the play.

Every word is placed to the best economy of the whole; the tone is grave, convincing, and the suggestions are so rich that we repeat the lines many times without exhausting their meaning. Suppose the poet had written:

> Life is a play at which the soul looks on,
> We must not judge it till the play is done.
> Her plot hath many changes; every day
> Speaks a new scene; the last act crowns the play.

We have not changed the poem very much, yet the small change we have made destroys all the beauty of it. In a short piece of this sort, we must be swung into the proper mood at the very first phrase; otherwise, the poem is over before we are in the right frame of mind.

To sum up: Definitions in verse should be sharp, compact, and memorable. It is better to suggest them than to state them, and after they are written, they

should be examined with critical eagerness to cut them
down to their shortest possible length.

IN THE DESERT

Sun tortured stillness wraps the trackless space,
The undulating sands, a muted sea,
Shift with each burning breath, uneasily,
The Yucca flower lifts a withered face
And roaming cattle parched, with weary pace
Have sought for drink, and dropped in agony;
The guardian mountains rise with majesty
The silent scions of a titan race;

But sunset draws her crimson veil at last
Across the golden armor of the West
And Evening comes with pity in her eyes,
The scorching anguish of the day is past
The fevered earth exhausted, sinks to rest,
The Desert clad in sackcloth, prostrate lies.

Let us pass over the ineffectual punctuation of these
verses, and the weak rhymes in the octave, to speak of
less apparent flaws.

The author has evidently felt his subject intensely.
He has been on the desert, it has moved him, and he
has wished to communicate his emotions to others.
What is his task, then? To choose from the pictures
those few which best summon the whole desert before
the mind of the reader, and to choose from his re-
sponsive moods just *one* to pull the sonnet together.
In his enthusiasm, however, he has not been selective.

He has wanted to include everything. Like a garrulous woman who can not leave untold a single phrase or trick of her amazing offspring, the poet confounds us with his eagerness. If we would find the symbol of this weakness, we should regard the adjectives. Whenever we find a writer unsatisfied with plain nouns, whenever we find him hanging an adjective or two on every noun he employs, then we know he is over-writing. *Stillness, space, sands*—these three words have more suggestion of the desert by themselves than when they are adorned with all those dead adjectives. Let the reader repeat them to himself several times and then, in comparison, read the first two lines of the sonnet, if he would perceive how much the author has weakened his subject by the additional words.

Now the overuse of adjectives is merely the symbol of the underlying fault of the sonnet. Let us examine the pictorial details and the metaphors. There are too many! Before one has taken possession of the imagination, another crowds it out. The figure of the desert as a muted sea is quite enough for a quatrain of the composition. The Yucca flower (*flower,* by the way, should occupy but one syllable) is out of place and wrenches the focus of the picture. Our eyes are looking afar over a muted sea of sand. They might well fasten themselves on a group of cattle or the distant mountains, but suddenly to thrust a Yucca flower before them produces a sad astigmatism. If the flower be important, our gaze might well draw inward slowly until, in the sestet, it come to rest on the Yucca, in which case the plant would receive tremendous emphasis (see Rossetti's "Woodspurge" once more). But as it stands, it has merely the effect of an item which the eager poet was unwilling to omit from his catalogue.

In the second quatrain, again, which should have the emphasis, the cattle or the mountains? The author has balanced them exactly; they are unrelated to each other, two more items of observation. If the cattle are to be the picture (and I think they ought to be), they should be brought out sharply against the mountainous horizon. And by all means, let us be rid of the eighth line, which is verbiage merely.

Unfortunately, the sestet begins where the octave left off: on the note of abstraction sounded by the eighth line. There is far too much apparel in this part of the poem. The veils, the armor, and the sackcloth are not true pictures nor are they effective metaphors. The author stopped feeling and seeing after his seventh line, and all the rest is "literature." Let him turn to Mr. Arthur Waley's translations of "170 Chinese Poems" for examples of fine mood-pictures. Simplicity! A spare economy, an unhesitant choice of the one image needed to stimulate the reader's imagination.

CHAPTER 11

ON READING VERSE ALOUD

Most readers of poetry perform by ear, and depend on the free dramatization of meaning or mood to carry them along. Since few have a good natural ear, the results are generally embarrassing to the audience. Not even poets themselves can, as a rule, manage their own cadences properly. They chant, vociferate, mumble, and grunt. The inner ear may have accomplished wonders of subtlety, but the outer fails to observe them.

The first obstacles to be overcome are self-consciousness and the consequent instinct to interpret rather than present the work. One should aim to be the bow in the master's hand—not the master himself. Any poem worthy the name has enough intensity within itself to obviate the need for dramatization. The reader should deliver himself up to the poem as its instrument. "Make me thy lyre!" Since poetry should never be chanted, pitch should be flexible. The two extremes to be avoided are "elocution" and singsong.

For more concise and definite principles we must penetrate the inmost shrine of Rhythm where pulse those mysterious forces which move beneath the flow

of English metre. Many prosodists have entered this
shrine never again to emerge into the sweet light of the
sun. Locked in mortal combat with each other, or lost
in the gigantic mazes of Theory, they sacrifice both life
and poetry.

First, we have the paradox of accent, or stress. Eng-
lish verse is indubitably based on a *theoretical* (but not
an actual) pattern of recurrent accent. An iambic pen-
tameter, we say, is a five-foot line, each foot containing
an unaccented, followed by an accented, syllable. It
would be difficult to find many such lines in the whole
range of English poetry, for our verse is based on recur-
rent accent as an iceberg is based on the larger part that
is submerged and invisible.

Much have / I trav / ell'd in / the realms / of gold.

Much and *trav* are full accents, but *much,* as I have
already pointed out, is theoretically in the wrong half
of the foot. *Realms* and *gold* are weaker accents. *In*
can not be accented at all. Thus we have an iambic
pentameter not with five, but with only two, primary
accents. Why, then, is such a line permissible?

Because the *time rhythm* darts back and forth in ever-
changing units to give balance to the line as a whole.
It shrinks where the accent is strong, and expands where
the accent is weak. In the line quoted above, *in* is not
adequate to the metrical place it occupies. Therefore
the time rhythm holds up the line with the long syl-
lables *realms* and *gold,* which compensate for the miss-

ing stress. Thus we have a constant interplay between accent and time, between strength and length, which, in spite of irregularity in detail, brings every line to a metrical balance. Time rhythm is like the spider alert to repair every rent in the symmetry of the web. Accent rhythm is the web itself. With due apologies to Keats, let us rewrite his line, substituting short syllables for his long ones. "Much have I travell'd in the infinite." It drops to pieces (as poetry of the "infinite" generally does).

This time rhythm works through two equally important elements. The first is called *duration,* and depends on the length or shortness of an individual syllable. *It* is short; *slow* is long; and between these extremes lie innumerable variations of swiftness or length. Although long durations are generally dependent on long vowel sounds, in words like *strength,* wherein the consonants draw out the sound, we find not only a full accent, but a long duration as well. The second element in time rhythm is a silence, a *pause.* Pause corresponds to the "rest" in music. It is essential that the reader of poetry consider both duration and pause with rapt attention. They are the time rhythm, time smoothing out the irregularities of accent. They must be over-observed. Their differences must be brought out far more emphatically than in the reading of prose. Also, acceleration is just as important as retard. Short syllables must be staccato, or the long can not fulfill their contrasting function. For practice, take Housman's line:—

The fleet foot × on the sill of shade.

It is as necessary to hurry over the quick syllables *on the* as to draw out the two equal longs *fleet foot*. Note, in passing, that only the word *sill* receives a full accent. An even more striking example is Bridges's

Ah × × soon × × × when Winter has all our vales
    opprest.

In this line the exceedingly long durations *ah* and *soon,* with their long attendant pauses, *are equal in time to the nine syllables which follow*. Only the first syllable of *Winter* and the second syllable of *opprest* receive a full accent. Yet in theory this is an iambic pentameter, scanned thus:—

Ah soon / when Win / ter has all / our vales / opprest.

It is apparent how widely divergent are the underlying metres and the actual sounds of English verse.

At this point the reader is doubtless wondering what he should do about the accent rhythm. We have agreed that beneath the surge and thunder of the time rhythm a regular, though submerged, accentual pattern sustains the verse. Let us change our original figure and compare the accent to a skeleton, which, though unseen, holds the anatomy to its proper form and proportion. We can always scan metrical verse accentually even if we do not read it according to the scansion. Such a metrical chart might be compared to an X-ray picture of the bony structure beneath the flesh. Even such a line as Milton's

Hail ho / ly Light / off spring / of Heav'n / first-born.

will submit to the investigation. In Shakspere's

In sooth / I know / not why / I am / so sad

the bony contour is nearer the surface. Poets often delight in conjoining fat and lean lines for the sake of variety. For practical performance, the reader should disregard accent, provided that he read naturally so that the accents fall into their normal places as they would in lively conversation. Accent is the essence of the English tongue, and may be left to take care of itself. It is impossible not to accent where an accent truly belongs. More often words are falsely accented because of their metrical position. This fault should be avoided. It would be impossible not to accent these lines properly:—

$\times$ $\times$ Break $\times$ $\times$ Break $\times$ $\times$ Break $\times$
on thy cold gray stones O Sea!

It is also very easy to overdo. Study the time units, the slow, the quick, the pause; then stress will assume its proper place. In the ordinary iambic pentameter, the average number of full stresses is not more than two.

Pitch presents a vaguer problem, because the raising or lowering of the voice varies with the individual. For example, a relative of mine used to start every sentence at the top of the scale, slide to the bottom about two thirds of the way through, and, at the end, slide halfway up again. A foreigner would have thought him in a perpetual state of questioning worry. For the most part, Americans do not avail themselves nearly enough of a changing pitch. They avoid it as an affectation and lose half the effectiveness of their native tongue in drone, drawl, and growl. Yet the American voice is, in general, far richer than the English. Leaving out Cockney,—and that super-Cockney, the "Oxford accent,"—we mistakenly accord superiority to the English *voice,* whereas actually the more flexible *pitch* gives the advantage. Pitch is to our tongue as hand-waving is to the French: its expressiveness, its emphasis, and its point. *Without sliding pitch the reading of verse can not be effective.* Yet I can not set any formula, or improvise a tune. I have noticed that, in moments of excitement, Americans lose their self-consciousness and sing out very well. Any good poem should arouse sufficient excitement to limber up the vocal chords. Away with constraint!

Enjambment (the overflow of one line into the next) is a problem which causes more confusion than pitch, yet has a clear solution. A large proportion of lines in English verse, especially in long poems and the drama, are locked together by their syntax: they "run over" into each other; they are "enjambed."

Thou by the Indian Ganges' side
Shouldst rubies find: I by the tide
Of Humber would complain. I would
Love you ten years before the Flood,
And you should, if you please, refuse
Till the conversion of the Jews.

In these lines of Marvell's, we note the sentence struc-
tures running through line after line, with no chance
for a pause to indicate the end of a line. The same de-
vice is common in blank verse. More than two thirds
of the lines in *Paradise Lost* are enjambed; and Shak-
spere, especially in his later plays, poured the lava of
his thought over long series of boundary walls. The
mishandling of Shakspere's enjambments is notori-
ous.

There are two wrong ways of treating this device
orally, and one right way. The poets themselves have
so clearly pointed out the right way that I fail to under-
stand how so many have missed it. The problem is this:
a sentence leaps from line to line, ignoring metrical
boundaries—how shall we preserve the integrity of the
individual lines without placing pauses where they do
not naturally occur? Or, on the other hand, preserve
the normal syntax without melting the lines together
into a formless mass? The old school of Shaksperean
actors declaimed the speeches by the line and imparted
a false rhetoric to the whole. The modern school fol-
lows the syntax merely and puts the poet to rout in
favor of the dramatist.

But no such dilemma exists. All poets, consciously or instinctively, have indicated the method to be employed in reading enjambment. In enjambed passages, every line that runs over into the next is terminated by a syllable with a long vowel or with consonants that can be extended. Here, then, is the rule: Draw out the last syllable of the first line; then, *without pause or change of pitch,* launch into the second line. Thus:—

> Thou by the Indian Ganges' side
> Shouldst rubies find: I by the tide
> Of Humber would complain. I would
> Love you ten years before the Flood,
> And you should, if you please, refuse
> Till the conversion of the Jews.

From what has been said so far, we may deduce the following principles for reading verse aloud:—

(1) Read out in a full but unstrained voice.

(2) Do not dramatize the poem.

(3) Do not chant it.

(4) Stress only the syllables that would be stressed in conversation; indeed, let the stress take care of itself.

(5) Read short syllables in a hurry and long ones at leisure.

(6) Observe all pauses extravagantly. Silence can never make a mistake.

(7) Vary the pitch eagerly.

(8) When lines overflow into each other, draw out the

last syllable of the overflowing line, and, without pause or change of pitch, collide with the first syllable of the line that follows.

These eight principles would be valueless without the ninth, which governs them all. The ninth is, quite literally, the heart of the matter, for its steady pulse sends life through all the veins of English verse. My discovery of it was a happy accident. For years I had been vaguely conscious of swaying backward and forward in time to the verse I was reading. A poem of great syllabic irregularity, Walter de la Mare's "Listeners," demanded an explanation of this weaving that evened out lines of very disproportionate length.

> "Is there anybody there?" said the Traveler,
> Knocking on the moonlit door.

Both the lines have three metrical feet, but the first line has twelve syllables, and the second, seven. Both of them divide into two equal time units; and these units are equal through the two lines and those that follow— in spite of the discrepancy in the number of syllables.

$$1 \qquad\qquad\qquad 2$$

Is there anybody there $|$ $\times$ $\times$ said the Traveler $\times$

$$1 \qquad\qquad\qquad 2$$

Knocking on the $\overline{\text{moon lit}}$ $|$ $\overline{\text{door.}}$ $\times$ $\times$

Continuing my experiment, I discovered the cardinal principle, the prime movement, of our verse. *All lines in English verse, more than one foot in length, divide into two equal time units. These units cut across feet, accent, syllables, and may even split a single word. More often than not, there is no pause between them.* Theoretically, then, the best way to read English verse is to a metronome. Practically, there are gradual accelerations and retards which change the general tempo, but never disorganize the equality of the two time units within the single line.

These two units are doubtless a survival from the prosody of our Anglo-Saxon ancestors. The Anglo-Saxon line broke into two equal time units, the only difference from our rhythm being that those units were always separated by a pause, whereas ours more frequently are not. It is not surprising that such a survival should prevail, for many more elements of our primitive verse remain than are generally recognized. There are lines in many modern poets, notably Meredith and Swinburne, which would fit Anglo-Saxon metrics perfectly.

The reason that this double metronomic rhythm does not become monotonous is that the number of syllables within the units constantly varies, along with the durations and the placing of the pauses.

The $\overline{\text{lone}} \times \overline{\text{couch}} \times \times$ | of his everlasting sleep.

In this line, three syllables balance against seven.

A good many consonants, such as *n, m, l,* and *ng,* have echoes which fill out a unit:—

$\overline{\text{Wake}} \times$ for the sun | has scattered into $\overline{\text{flight}}$.

Note how the two long syllables *Wake* and *flight* balance the two ends of the line.

When two similar consonants collide at the end of one word and the beginning of another, a pause is demanded to avoid running the two words together.

$$\overline{\text{While}}\ \text{she}\ \overline{\text{lies}} \times |$$
$$\text{Sleep}\breve{\text{ing.}} \times$$

As I have said, the units sometimes meet in the middle of a word, as in the first of these two lines:—

Where in her Mediterran | ean mirror gazing
Old Asia's dreamy face × | wrinkleth to a westward smile.

By way of final illustration, let us divide an entire poem into its time units. Fearful that my colleagues in the art might object if one of their productions were thus anatomized, I offer up a lyric of my own for vivisection. (Let no saucy reader substitute the word *autopsy*.)

Note well that, though I have had to divide each line to denote the two units, there should be no pause between them unless a pause is indicated.

NIGHT PIECE

There is always the sound	|	of falling water here,
By day, blended with	|	birdsong and windy leaves,
By night, the only sound,	× |	steady and clear
Through the darkness and half-	|	heard through sleepers' dreams.
Here in the mottled shadow	|	of glades, the deer
Unstartled, waits	× |	until the walker is near,
Then with a silent bound,	| ×	without effort is gone,
While the sound of falling wa	|	ter goes on and on.

Those are not stars | reflected in the lake,
They are shadow of stars | that were there æons ago;
When you walk by these waters | at night, you must forsake
All you have known of time; | ✕ you are timeless, alone,
The mystery almost revealed | like the breath you take
In the summer dawn ✕ | before the world is awake,
Or the last breath | ✕ when the spirit beyond recalling
Goes forth to the sound | of water forever falling.

Swift as deer, ✕ | half-thoughts in the summer mind
Flash with their hints of | happiness and are gone;
In the dark waters | ✕ of ourselves we find
No stars but shadows | of stars which memory lost.
Dark are the waters | under the bridge we crossed,
And the sound of their falling | knows neither end nor start.
Frail are your stars, | ✕ deep are your waters, mind;
And the sound of falling | water troubles my heart.

A SELECTED READING LIST

ANTHOLOGIES generally available throughout the libraries of the country and of proved merit are the OXFORD BOOK OF ENGLISH VERSE (Revised Edition, edited by Quiller-Couch) and the combined volume of MODERN AMERICAN POETRY and MODERN BRITISH POETRY edited by Louis Untermeyer. The student will find examples of the various forms treated in this book and will equip himself with a basic selection of good lyric poetry by familiarizing himself with these two volumes, and especially with the following selections:

From the *Oxford Book:*

The Early Anonymous Poems.
Poems by Geoffrey Chaucer.
Numbers from Elizabethan Miscellanies and Song Books by Unnamed or Uncertain Authors.
Poems by Sir Walter Raleigh, Edmund Spenser, Sir Philip Sidney, George Peele, Samuel Daniel, Michael Drayton, William Shakspere, Thomas Campion, Ben Jonson, John Donne, John Webster, Robert Herrick, George Herbert, John Milton, Andrew Marvell, Henry Vaughan.
Ballads and Songs by Unknown Authors.
Poems by John Dryden, Matthew Prior, Alexander

Pope, Thomas Gray, William Collins, William Blake, William Wordsworth, Samuel Taylor Coleridge, Walter Savage Landon, Lord Byron, Percy Bysshe Shelley, John Keats, Lord Tennyson, Robert Browning, Matthew Arnold, Dante Gabriel Rossetti, George Meredith, Algernon Charles Swinburne.

From *Modern British Poetry:*

Poems by Thomas Hardy, Austin Dobson, Oscar Wilde, Gerard Manley Hopkins, Robert Bridges, A. E. Housman, William Butler Yeats, Lionel Johnson, Walter de la Mare, John Masefield, James Stephens, Arthur Waley, Rupert Brooke, W. H. Auden, Stephen Spender.

From *Modern American Poetry:*

Poems by Emily Dickinson, George Santayana, Edwin Arlington Robinson, Robert Frost, Vachel Lindsay, William Rose Benét, T. S. Eliot, Conrad Aiken, Stephen Vincent Benét, Robert Hillyer, Maria Zarurenska.

(N.B. It will be noted that this reading list omits the names of poets who are not illustrative of fundamental principles of metric, even though they may be important from other points of view. The reader should explore the collections further on his own initiative.)

ILLUSTRATIVE READING FOR
SPECIFIC CHAPTERS

Chapter 1: *Oxford Book:* Poems by Andrew Marvell, Thomas Gray, Dante Gabriel Rossetti.

Modern British Poetry: Poems by Thomas Hardy, Robert Bridges, A. E. Housman.

Modern American Poetry: Poems by Emily Dickinson, Edwin Arlington Robinson, Robert Frost.

Chapter 2: *Oxford Book:* The Early Anonymous Poems, Numbers from Elizabethan Miscellanies, Poems by Edmund Spenser, William Shakspere, Thomas Campion, William Blake, Lord Byron, Percy Bysshe Shelley, John Keats, Lord Tennyson, Algernon Charles Swinburne.

Modern British Poetry: Poems by William Butler Yeats, James Stephens.

Modern American Poetry: Poems by Vachel Lindsay, Conrad Aiken.

Chapter 3: *Oxford Book:* Poems by Michael Drayton, John Donne, John Milton, Samuel Taylor Coleridge.

Modern British Poetry: Poems by Gerard Manley Hopkins, Walter de la Mare, James Stephens.

Modern American Poetry: Poems by Robert Frost, Stephen Vincent Benét, Robert Hillyer, Maria Zaturenska.

Chapter 4: *Oxford Book:* Poems by Geoffrey Chaucer, Edmund Spenser, Ben Jonson, Robert Herrick, John Dryden, Matthew Prior, Alexander Pope, Thomas Gray, Walter Savage Landor, Percy Bysshe Shelley, John Keats, Matthew Arnold.

Modern British Poetry: Poems by A. E. Housman, John Masefield.

Chapter 5: *Oxford Book:* Sonnets by Edmund Spenser, Sir Philip Sidney, Samuel Daniel, Michael Drayton, William Shakspere, John Donne, John Milton, William Wordsworth, John Keats, Matthew Arnold, George Meredith.

Modern British Poetry: Sonnets by Robert Bridges, Rupert Brooke.

Modern American Poetry: Sonnets by George Santayana, Edwin Arlington Robinson, Robert Hillyer.

Chapter 6: *Modern British Poetry:* Poems by Austin Dobson, Oscar Wilde.

Modern American Poetry: E. A. Robinson, "The House on the Hill."

Chapter 7: *Oxford Book:* Odes by Ben Jonson, John Milton, Andrew Marvell, John Dryden, Thomas Gray, William Collins, William Wordsworth, Percy Bysshe Shelley, John Keats.

INDEX